MY SACRIFICE, HIS FIRE

OTHER BOOKS BY RAY AND ANNE ORTLUND

Anne Ortlund, *Up with Worship*, Regal Books (what should happen between your ears on a Sunday morning).

Anne Ortlund, *Disciplines of the Beautiful Woman*, Word Publishing (life management through a notebook, desk, wardrobe, etc.).

Anne Ortlund, *Disciplines of the Heart*, Word Publishing (on a woman's inner life).

Anne Ortlund, *Disciplines of the Home*, Word Publishing (on family life together).

Anne Ortlund, *Discipling One Another*, Word Publishing ("how to's" for small fellowship groups).

Anne Ortlund, *Children Are Wet Cement*, Baker Books (handling children; Christy Award for best marriage-family book of 1982).

Anne Ortlund, *Joanna: A Story of Renewal*, Word Publishing (Anne's first fiction).

Anne Ortlund, *Building a Great Marriage*, Baker Books (for any age but especially early marriage).

Anne Ortlund, *Fix Your Eyes on Jesus* (practical ways to stay Christ-centered).

Raymond C. and Anne Ortlund, *The Best Half of Life*, Word Publishing (for age thirty-five and beyond: money, marriage, goals, etc.).

Raymond C. and Anne Ortlund, *You Don't Have to Quit*, Oliver-Nelson (perseverance in marriage, job, school, relationships, etc.).

Raymond C. and Anne Ortlund, *Confident in Christ*, Questar Publishing (what it means to be in Christ—its privileges, its responsibilities).

Raymond C. Ortlund, *Intersections*, Word Publishing (studies in the Gospel of Luke).

Raymond C. Ortlund, *Three Priorities for a Strong Local Church*, Word Publishing (for pastors and lay leaders).

Raymond C. Ortlund, *Lord, Make My Life a Miracle*, Regal Books (priorities to live by).

Anne Ortlund

MY SACRIFICE, HIS FIRE

Weekday Readings for Women

WORD PUBLISHING
Dallas • London • Vancouver • Melbourne

Unless otherwise indicated, all Scripture references are from the New International Version of the Bible, copyright © 1978 by the New York International Bible Society; used by permission.

Other Scripture quotations are from the following sources:

> The King James Version of the Bible (KJV). The Living Bible (TLB), copyright 1971 by Tyndale House Publishers, Wheaton, Illinois. The New American Standard Bible (NASB) © 1960, 1962, 1963, 1968, 1971, 1972, 1973, 1975, 1977 by The Lockman Foundation. Used by permission. The New King James (NKJV), copyright © 1979, 1980, 1982, Thomas Nelson, Inc., Publishers. Used by permission. The New Testament in Modern English (PHILLIPS) by J. B. Phillips, published by The MacMillan Company © 1958, 1960, 1972 by J. B. Phillips.

The author extends thanks to the following publishers for permission to reprint from these books:

> *Confident in Christ*, 1989, Questar Publishing, Sisters, Oregon.
> *You Don't Have to Quit*, 1993, Thomas Nelson, Nashville, Tennessee.
> *Up with Worship*, 1975, Regal Books, Ventura, California.
> *Building a Great Marriage*, 1985, and *Children Are Wet Cement*, 1981, Baker Books, Grand Rapids, Michigan.
> *Women's Devotional Bible*, 1990, Zondervan Corporation, Grand Rapids, Michigan.

Amy Carmichael's poem, "Light in the Cell," is reprinted with permission from *Toward Jerusalem*, 1936, 1977, published by Christian Literaure Crusade. Used by permission.

"Turn Your Eyes upon Jesus," copyright 1922, renewed 1950 by H. H. Lemmel. Assigned to Singspiration Music/ASCAP. All rights reserved. Used by permission of Benson Music Group, Inc.

"Think of It, Lord," by Anne Ortlund © 1971, 1973 Singspiration, a division of the Zondervan Corporation. All rights reserved. Used by permission.

Library of Congress Cataloging-in-Publication Data

Ortlund, Anne.
    My sacrifice, his fire : weekday readings for women / Anne Ortlund.
        p.   cm.
    Includes bibliographical references.
    ISBN 0–8499–1070–6
    1. Women, Christian—Prayer-books and devotionals—English.   2. Devotional calendars.   I. Title.
BV4844.O77   1993
242'.643—dc20   93–17924
                                                                          CIP

3 4 5 6 9   BVG   9 8 7 6 5 4 3 2

Printed in the United States of America

To Melinda

co-worker and friend,
who through severe pregnancy nausea
faithfully word processed this manuscript,
while living its truths before me daily . . .
with gratitude, admiration and affection

Contents

Foreword

Today the LORD will appear to you. (Lev. 9:4)

As you peruse these readings each weekday for the next year, I am praying that He will indeed appear to you!

Leviticus 9 tells the story of the first time the Israelite priests ever ministered.

The gorgeous tabernacle had been finished at last (Exodus 36–39).

Aaron, the first high priest, and his sons had gotten their final instructions concerning the offerings (Leviticus 1–7).

Then they'd taken baths, for the first time put on their beautiful robes, and been ordained. And then, at God's command, they'd simply stayed at the tabernacle's entrance, where all could see that they were just being quiet. One daily sacrifice, one altar anointing. Otherwise, nothing. They waited a whole week! They waited in expectation for the Big Day.

It came. And as that special morning dawned, the Lord said to Aaron, and through him to the people, "Today the LORD will appear to you."

"Today"!

9

The entire assembly of Israelites gathered, to watch and worship. Aaron and his boys offered the sacrifices.

> *Whack!* They slaughtered a calf.
> *Splat!* They sprinkled blood on the altar's horns.
> *Swish.* They washed the animal's inner parts and legs.
> *Work. Grunt. Sweat.*

So far, human people had been doing the only parts that human people can do—work, ritual, rest, more work—in spiritual weakness but in obedience, as best they knew how.

. . . And then suddenly

SWOOSH!! SIZZLE!! LIGHT!! HEAT!!

"Fire came out from the presence of the LORD and consumed the burnt offering. . . .

"And when all the people saw it, they shouted for joy and fell face downward" (Lev. 9:24).

Oh, my friend! I've done my human, impotent work of sacrifice, at Word Publishing's request, to gather excerpts from my twelve books and arrange them into daily readings.

Now you do your human work of sacrifice to set yourself to a weekday reading schedule. And then—will He send His fire?

Look for Him!

Look for Him to appear to you.

Maybe today!

Anne Ortlund
Newport Beach, California

*T*here you are, a woman—how wonderful! How unique you are, not "made in Japan" but made in your mother's womb. A factory needs plenty of light; God was so smart He could make you perfectly in the dark.

That cowlick of yours, the length of your toes, your upper lip—He made all of you, and you are therefore very special and precious. (I'm unique, too. Children are amazed to see the crack right down the center of my tongue; I've never seen another tongue like it!)

Disciplines of the Beautiful Woman

There are more than five billion people on this planet, and there's no one like you—nor has there ever been, nor will there ever be. You are His precious, one-of-a-kind treasure. Do you really believe that? Said William Ellery Channing (1780–1842), "Every human is intended to have a character of his own; to be what no others are, and to do what no other can do." From the very beginning, when you were only a much-loved concept in God's mind, you've been a combination of materials like nobody else.

Don't shrink from being what you are. Ethel Waters used to say, "God don't sponsor no flops!"

Accept your limitations light-heartedly. He made you exactly right. Are you below par in some way? Read Exodus 4:11 and John 9:1–3 and believe with joy.

Accept your strengths, too, with humility and gratitude. He knew what He was doing when He put you together. Assess yourself "with sober judgment, in accordance with the measure of faith God has given you" (Rom. 12:3).

Assess yourself honestly, and then—

Live in the sunshine! Abide in Him. Stay in your Lover's love (John 15:9) and don't wander out of it.

Disciplines of the Heart

11

What consumes you? *What is your passion? Where are you going? Have you pinpointed your aim? Does your life have a specific target?*

You know, deep inside, what you need: *Fix your eyes on Jesus.*

Whatever your lifestye, your situation, your connections—first of all, most of all, fix your eyes on Him. *Dedicate yourself to make Him your focus. Let all your other loves flow out of that.*

You'll grow downward and upward and outward—but you'll always be stable, centralized, focused, balanced.

Jesus Himself

        strengthens your weaknesses,

        tones down your excesses,

        brings your under-normals up to normal and makes your above-normals not seem overpowering and intimidating,

        refines what is crude,

        helps the rigid to relax,

        helps the over-polished to loosen up,

        helps the lowly born to get "class."

Some people don't want to fix their eyes on Jesus; they imagine that would make them religious freaks. Listen:

> *Jesus Christ is the only One Who is perfectly whole and healthy and balanced and normal. And the more you fix your eyes on Him, the more whole and healthy and balanced and normal you will be.*

Fix Your Eyes on Jesus

12

*W*illiam Law around 1750 said everyone fixes his eyes on something; he interpreted that as "praying without ceasing." He said people pray continually as long as they're alive, because it's part of human nature.

> The [person] whose heart habitually tends toward the riches, honors, powers or pleasures of this life, is in a continual state of prayer toward all these things. His spirit stands always bent towards them. They have his hope, his love, his faith, and are . . . in reality the God of his heart.*

Can't you see that whatever we think is lacking or in short supply in our life, we could easily "pray without ceasing" toward that?

> in a jail cell, pray without ceasing toward release;
> in poverty, pray toward money;
> under an oppressive government, toward freedom;
> in loneliness, toward companionship. . . .

All the milling peoples of the world, each lacking *something*, can fix their eyes on their particular lack and be always restless, complaining, ungrateful, unhappy.

In your good times, in your bad times, when life is wonderful, when life is awful—don't fix your eyes on your life, fix your eyes on Jesus.

I'm writing more than I've attained, but it both motivates me and stabilizes me to read this other quotation from that same remarkable William Law, written also around 1750: "The pious soul that eyes only God . . . can have no stop in its progress; light and darkness equally assist him. In the light he looks up to God. In the darkness he lays hold of God, and so they both do him the same good."†

Fix Your Eyes on Jesus

---

*William Law, *A Serious Call to a Devout and Holy Life*.
†Ibid.

*T*hink *of a sponge plunged into the ocean.* It soaks up the sea water until it's totally saturated. Still—it's still a sponge.

Think of yourself, fixing your eyes on Jesus. You're plunged into an awareness of His presence, surrounding you wherever you go. You "soak up" the Lord and all His characteristics until you're saturated. And yet you're still you.

But this habit doesn't just "happen": *It begins with desire, and it continues with discipline.* It's not just automatic, it's *learned*—like somebody's being initiated into a fraternity or sorority, until they're at last in the fellowship:

> Blessed are those who have learned to acclaim you
> > who walk in the light of your presence, O LORD.
> They rejoice in your name all the day long;
> > they exult in your righteousness.
> For you are their glory and strength. (Ps. 89:15–17)

The ocean becomes the sponge's very own watery-ness and saltiness.

The Lord becomes *your very own* glory and strength. You receive all your achievements, your happiness, your wellbeing from what is continually surrounding you: the presence of God Himself. You're soaking Him up!

Then start right now. And check in ten minutes from now, and ten minutes after that . . . *The presence of God in your life will become your glory and your strength.*

Moses insisted on it (Exod. 33:15).

David wouldn't live without it (Ps. 27:8).

Fix Your Eyes on Jesus

*L*et every part of your life—your person, your style, your direction, your flavor—be in Him. When you're in Him, then you're based on truth. You'll be honest and genuine through and through; you'll be coordinated, all of a piece; you'll be in harmony with yourself. And then you can grow within yourself to unlimited dimensions—and all because you're in God.

Faddish lives age quickly. They're not based on God, who is greater than all culture and all generations, so twenty years from now they'll seem faded and "out of it." Anchor yourself to the great "I AM," and you will develop more and more into a woman who is ageless, whole, true, and at rest.

When you abide in Him, when you truly focus on Him until you specialize, then that kind of centeredness and concentration will cause something remarkable to emerge. In the "specializing" God will accent the "special"! You won't just be living in the sunshine, but you yourself will have taken on characteristics of the sun.

God will be developing in you the power to radiate and affect things and structures and people.

Truth is so powerful! Righteousness is so dynamic! Get on your face before Him and surrender yourself to Him, that this might be so.

Disciplines of the Heart

> God . . . acts on behalf of those who wait for him. (Isa. 64:4)

Υou can put your trust in the Source of all staying power, God Himself.

What a God!

Moses asked Him what His name was, and He answered, "I AM."

"I AM." Simple. Direct. Unequivocal. There is no hesitation, no hint of not-having-quite-arrived, no exaggeration.

"I AM." Positive. Assured. Self-validated. He is alive and well, and not to be questioned.

"I AM." Current. Continuous. There is no apology, no explanation, no contextualizing.

"I AM." Complete. Self-contained. Secure.

"I AM." Unique. Other. Transcendent.

"I AM." What He is, He is; what He chooses to be, He will be. . . . He is THE NAME: "I AM."*

And centuries after He gave us that Name, He stooped to reveal Himself in terms we better understand: time terms. He said, "I am He 'who was and who is, and who is to come.'" (See Rev. 1:4.)

"So I understand your past and your present and your future. I identify with you in each. And I have ultimate staying power: I am the same yesterday, today, and forever."

Let your life be settled on this great surety, more than on any other support or concern: on God Himself.

You Don't Have to Quit

---

*Source Unknown.

16

*H*ave you thought about what awesome and exquisite *fun* is possible, the more you fix your eyes on Jesus? You understand more and more His love, His compassion, His grace, and His graciousness to *you.*

And you begin to realize just how forgiven and how eagerly received by Him you really are!

So many Christians live essentially apart from Him—officially connected but not enjoying Him at all. They stay aloof because they don't understand *what He's really like.*

When He's in the company of His dear ones *He loves to party.* That's what He's like!

Moses and the other spiritual leaders of Israel "went up and saw the God of Israel"—*gulp!*—and "they ate and drank" (Exod. 24:9–11)!

King David and his people faithfully sacrificed to atone for their sins, and then "they ate and drank with great joy in the presence of the LORD" (1 Chron. 29:22).

The prodigal son got sick of his waywardness and repented and came home, and his father provided great new clothes for him, a new ring, and a dinner party with music and dancing (Luke 15:22–25).

You see, it's only a Christian's own attitude that causes any blockage. When you asked God to forgive you and save you, from that moment on *He doesn't hold anything further against you. He doesn't count your sins against you anymore.*

If you're a believer—if you're "in Christ"—then kick up your heels! Celebrate the Lord! Celebrate yourself! Discover a life of pleasure you never dreamed possible.

> Let all who take refuge in [the Lord] be glad;
>   let them ever sing for joy. (Ps. 5:11)

> Rejoice in the Lord always. (Phil. 4:4)

Fix Your Eyes on Jesus

17

OMNIPRESENCE

I WALKED the other day along a river
And watched the ducks and heard some
        hawklings' cries;
Then suddenly the nearness of my Saviour
Brought tears of joy and wonder to my eyes.

    Oh, praise the Lord—
        "This earth is crammed with heaven"!
    Oh, praise the Lord—
        And, Christian, look around!
    For every bush you pass with fire is flaming,
    And every spot you tread is holy ground.

I stopped the other day to watch a fountain
And marveled at the magic of its grace;
Then suddenly my heart was on a mountain
And worshiping Jehovah face to face! . . .

I wept the other day—oh, Christian, hear it—
I wept the other day without control,
But suddenly the blessed Holy Spirit
Spoke peace again and calmed my needy soul.

    Oh, praise the Lord—
        "This earth is crammed with heaven"!
    Oh, praise the Lord—
        And, Christian, look around!
    For every bush you pass with fire is flaming,
    And every spot you tread is holy ground.
                    —*Anne Ortlund*

             Women's Devotional Bible

*H*ave you ever thought what it would be like to live in a one-dimensional world? It would be living along a straight line, and you could only travel between you and your nearest neighbor because you'd have no idea to step *off* the line and *go around*. There would be no "around" and two-dimensional people would look at you in pity because you had to live your whole life along one dull line.

Still, two-dimensional people are limited, too, aren't they? They know north and south and east and west—and maybe they think they've "arrived." They might say, "We can go west by southwest, or north by northeast, or anywhere we want!"

But they are flatlanders—unconsciously depressed by gravity and knowing only the horizontal outlook. They have no idea of "up" and "down"—and they don't even know they're missing anything.

Non-Christians, it seems to me, are one-dimensional people. They're lonely little dots, little islands of me-ism, of self-love, of self-preoccupation of every kind. Their challenge in life is to get farther along their one-dimensional line to more money, more power, and so on. The only way they see to do that is to knock off the line the people ahead of them who are blocking the way to their goals. Carnal Christians have the same mind-set; you can hardly tell the difference.

Lots more Christians are flatlanders. They talk about the Body and missions and about spiritual gifts and evangelism. And they may have no idea, either, that they're missing anything.

Oh, when Christians learn *up!*

Up is enlarging and releasing and purifying. *Up* is beyond atmospheric dust and smog; it's vast and limitless and beautiful. It's beyond committees and pecking orders and the push-pull of imperfect communications. *Up* has thrones and rainbows and morning stars singing together.

Up is the Big Picture. *Up* is communing with God Himself!

Up with Worship

19

Prayer:

O Lord Jesus Christ,
　　John saw You among the lampstands,
　　　　with Your face shining like the sun in
　　　　　　all its brilliance,
　　　　and Your voice like the sound of
　　　　　　rushing waters,
　　　　and seven stars in Your right hand.

I can't imagine how beautiful You must be.
　　A rainbow encircles You,
　　and before You is a sea of glass . . .
　　　　an exquisitely pure reflecting
　　　　　　pool . . .
　　　　　　doubling all Your splendor.

I see flashes of lightning from Your throne;
　　I hear exploding peals of thunder;
　　　　I smell heavenly incense from the
　　　　　　golden bowls . . .
My senses are dazzled.

　　"How handsome you are, my lover!
　　　　Oh, how charming!" (Song of Sol. 1:16)

Almost without breath,
　　"lost in wonder, love, and praise,"
　　　　I fix my eyes on You.

　　　　　　　　　Fix Your Eyes on Jesus

*W*hat is a beautiful woman? Only once does the Bible say it just like that: "beautiful woman." The words refer to Sarah, Abraham's wife, in Genesis 12:11, and literally they mean "a woman of beautiful appearance." We know that she was still alluring to men at the age of ninety; she was some woman, physically! And yet she laughed at God's words of the promise of a son in disbelief and then lied, denying it. And she was jealous of her maid. So physical beauty can't be everything.

In fact, when Proverbs 31 describes an admirable woman, her good qualities seem to be in opposition to physical beauty: "Charm is deceitful, and beauty is fleeting, but a woman who fears the LORD is to be praised" (Prov. 31:30).

But the New Testament seems to put it all together by suggesting that the godly woman does give an illusion of outward beauty:

> Your beauty should not come from outward adornment, such as braided hair and the wearing of gold jewelry and fine clothes. Instead, it should be that of your inner self, the unfading beauty of a gentle and quiet spirit, which is of great worth in God's sight. For this is the way the holy women of the past who put their hope in God used to make themselves beautiful. (1 Pet. 3:3–5)

When you "put your hope in God" you're not even aware of your own beauty, or lack of it; your focus is on Him. Godless women rely on a mirror; but you will *become a mirror:* reflecting the Lord's glory unselfconsciously, while being transformed into His likeness with ever-increasing glory (2 Cor. 3:18).

No wonder the Proverbs 31 woman "can laugh at the days to come"!

Disciplines of the Beautiful Woman

21

*I*f your environment is serene but your heart is not, you lose; isn't that true?

Right now, eliminate from mind even the closest circle surrounding you, and concentrate on your soul. Surrender to God. Relax; sink down into His terms. Let Him create in your spirit beauty and peace and rest.

> Hidden in the hollow
>   Of His blessed hand,
> Never foe can follow,
>   Never traitor stand;
> Not a surge of worry,
>   Not a shade of care,
> Not a blast of hurry
>   Touch the spirit there.
> Stayed upon Jehovah,
>   Hearts are fully blest;
> Finding, as he promised,
>   Perfect peace and rest.*

Now you may be joining Madame Jeanne Guyon and Mother Teresa and many others—women who through the centuries have lived in loveliness and peace and power without depending on any exterior at all. They've moved in beauty even in prisons and slums! Even if their most intimate surroundings have been beyond their control, in their hearts has been elegance and rest and God Himself.

Disciplines of the Heart

---

*Frances R. Havergal (1836–1879), "Like a River Glorious."

No longer be infants. . . . Instead, . . . grow up into
him who is the Head, that is, Christ. (Eph. 4:14–15)

*E*xpect to graduate out of the baby stage. Look forward to
moving beyond copying others to a wonderfully mature knowledge of God and His Word—and friendship with Him—that
will bring you into your own focus and style.

Look forward to becoming *only what you are*. (Then you
can really contribute to this world, because nobody else is what
you are.)

As your eyes are fixed on Jesus Christ, you'll find yourself
shedding what no longer represents you, what is inconsistent or
superfluous. It will happen. Said Richard of St. Victor long ago,
"The essence of purification is self-simplification."*

You'll find that you're deliberately unifying your life, your
person, your style, your interests, your flavor, your thrust. God
is One, and in Him you will discover more and more your own
inner integration and coherence and order.

Maxie Dunnam wrote,

Isn't this our desire: to move through our days not as pro-
grammed and driven machines but as deciding, creating persons? Don't we want to be centers of spiritual power and
harmony, having at least hints of life infused with and em-
powered by a sense of the Divine Presence?†

Disciplines of the Heart

---

*Quoted by Evelyn Underhill in *Mount of Purification*.
†Maxie Dunnam, *The Workbook of Spiritual Disciplines*.

Come unto me, all ye that labour and are heavy laden. . . . My burden is light. (Matt. 11:28–30 KJV)

*H*ow much emotional energy do you spend protecting yourself from every possible slight, challenging every word spoken by either friend or enemy which demeans you, cringing under every cool look, tossing at night because someone else seemed preferred over you? How much emotional energy do you spend trying to doctor up your image and "look good," trying to say only what's "cool," trying to do only what's accepted, trying to appear only in a way that will make you admired, trying to sustain a subtle publicity campaign that says you are more, do more, have more . . . ?

Exhausting, isn't it? It's a cruel, crushing burden, and it never lets up. It never lets you relax a minute to recoup. It wears away your strength, your morale, your life. We can call it "stress," but its real name is "ego."

Ego may be open or subtle, worldly or Christianized. It may mean smashing enough faces and brains to wow the world of boxing. It may mean taking over enough companies to wow the corporate world of business. It may mean getting enough church members to wow the religious world. Or individually, memorizing the most verses, visiting the most shut-ins, teaching the biggest Bible class—whatever makes the rest say "wow!"

Or ego may mean writhing and seething because you *haven't* made it to the top: you lost the match, your company was outclassed, your ministry is struggling. . . . Ego keeps you forever tense and dissatisfied, forever in agony lest someone else appear better, smarter, richer, more liked, more successful, more admired, more spiritual, more "blessed." . . .

Ego is a terrible, terrible burden.

Jesus says, "Let Me give you rest. Learn of Me. I am meek— and My burden is light."

Disciplines of the Heart

*R*emember, for all your adult life you'll be a woman. And how you live your life as a woman, all by yourself before God, is what makes the real you. Nothing on the exterior can touch or change that precious inner sanctuary—your heart, His dwelling place—unless you let it. And God, who loves you very much, has tailor made all your outer life—your circumstances, your relationships—to pressure you into becoming that beautiful woman He's planned for you to be.

How much of His planning will you accept? Your expectations for yourself should be enormous!

Second Kings 4 tells a story which illustrates the difference high expectations can make. It's about a widow with a big debt, who got the news that her creditor was going to take her two sons as payment of her debt!

The poor woman was beside herself, and she cried to Elisha, the man of God. His answer was, "Go borrow from your neighbors every container for oil that you can get. Don't borrow just a few."

The woman borrowed—and poured. From her scanty little supply she poured and poured. When all the containers were full, she said to her son, "Bring me another one." "That's all we have," he said—and with that the oil stopped.

Now, the oil she'd poured so far not only paid off her debt but kept her and her sons for life! But it was up to the woman how literally she obeyed Elisha to get many containers. If she had taken his words even more seriously she could have filled thousands of pots, and from then on fed the poor, donated large sums to the temple, and given herself and her sons every advantage. *Her expectation level determined her lifestyle, forever afterward.*

Lift up your eyes. Your heavenly Father waits to bless you in inconceivable ways to make your life what you never dreamed it could be.

Disciplines of the Beautiful Woman

*T*rue Christianity costs. It costs plenty. You kick out all the enemies. You put to death everything God tells you to put to death.

Lust must go—*wham!*

Greed, likewise—*pow!*

Filthy language isn't funny—*kill it!*

And if any of these enemies comes to and raises his head, bash him again.

To love God and to please Him is worth everything, everything. Your sexual immorality must go, your malice must go, your slander must go. All of them must go—forever! Be ruthless. Whatever the sins are that right now make you feel guilty and uneasy—hate them! Murder them! Get them once and for all out of your life.

And don't you dare read these words just to have read one more Christian book—just for a little evangelical tickling and entertainment. Let these words jar you to instant obedience.

What lurking thing are you hosting, coddling, hanging on to, putting up with? You know how your Christ feels about it.

You say you're "only a woman," and it doesn't even seem ladylike to think so tough?

General Sisera was an enemy of God, the commander of a Canaanite army which cruelly abused God's people, Israel. So Jael—"only a woman," "just a housewife"—lured him into her tent, offered him rest and a snack, got him covered up and cozy and off to sleep, quietly picked up a tent peg and a hammer, and—*THUNG!* She drove that thing right through his temple (Judg. 4:4–21).

You know what sin you have to put to death.

Do it with all your strength.

Personally.

Quickly.

Disciplines of the Heart

26

*B*ecome as a little child. Confess to Him that you're weak, you're foolish, you're penniless, you're unlearned, you're unskilled, you're uncouth—you're everything a child is.

Confess to Him your absolute and final inadequacy in yourself.

If you want to begin to experience His lifting and renewal, it's the only way. The way to up is down!

> For this is what the high and lofty One says—
>   he who lives forever, whose name is holy:
> "I live in a high and holy place,
>   but also with him who is contrite and lowly in
>   spirit,
> to revive the spirit of the lowly
>   and to revive the heart of the contrite."
>   (Isa. 57:15)

> The sacrifices of God are a broken spirit;
>   a broken and contrite heart,
>   O God, you will not despise. (Ps. 51:17)

Expose to Him all your deficiencies. Jesus loved the man who prayed, "Lord, be merciful to me, a sinner."

I say it, too, as I write these words.

> Repent, then, and turn to God, so that your sins may be wiped out, that times of refreshing may come from the Lord. (Acts 3:19)

Children Are Wet Cement

*N*els came back earlier this week from a five-day camp for the church high-schoolers. God had touched him in a real way, and as we drove along in the car he told us about a late-night experience of going out alone to cry bitterly over his sins. It's so special to have your big teenager willing to bare his soul, and I figured the best way to receive his story was to answer in kind.

"Boy, Nels," I said. "That was heavy, wasn't it! God does that to me sometimes, too. He got to me recently when I saw how arrogant I can be. I can act as if I have all the answers, and I don't realize at all how hard I am to live with. But God loves me so much, He'll bring along some experience, and pow! I see myself, and He brings me up short, and I bawl like a baby. He's not through with me yet, but He's helping me."

Now, in our family, that's meaningful sharing. And you can't schedule it or program it; you just have to be exposed to each other enough so that when God's time is right, you've got those precious moments to be real with each other.

And that's how it is in our spiritual family. James 5:16 says, "Therefore confess your sins to each other and pray for each other so that you may be healed." Our Roman Catholic friends have a weekly session with the priest, so that confession is automatically built into their lives; but when do we Protestants ever confess? We sin regularly; we should confess regularly, and stay continually cleaned out and forgiven.

Discipling One Another

> If we confess our sins, he is faithful and just and will forgive
> us our sins and purify us from all unrighteousness.
> (1 John 1:9)

*F*or most of us who live in cities, garbage gets collected once or twice a week. Do you remember what happened a few years ago when New York City had a garbage collectors' strike? How the stuff piled up! And as long as the temperature stayed below freezing it wasn't too bad, but when it thawed . . . That's the way many Christians are inside, because it's been so long since sins were confessed!

To whom do we confess? James 5:16 says "to each other"— Christians to Christians.

But when and where? It usually isn't too appropriate to pop up in church between the announcements and the offering. This is a crucial reason for small groups! The whole family of God can get totally clogged with unconfessed sins unless each member has a select group of brothers and sisters around him to whom he can relate in meaningful ways.

Ross Foley, in his book *You Can Win Over Weariness*, says that "professional listeners" can't help us too much because our confession to them is secret! He quotes a contemporary psychologist, O. Hobart Mowrer, who writes,

> I am persuaded that healing and redemption depend much more upon what we say about ourselves *to others, significant others*, than upon what others (no matter how highly trained or untrained, ordained or unordained) say *to us*.
>
> It's the truth we ourselves speak, rather than the treatment we receive, that heals us.*
>
> *Discipling One Another*

Then Nathan said to David, " . . . Why did you despise the word of the LORD by doing what is evil in his eyes? . . ."
Then David said to Nathan, "I have sinned against the LORD." (2 Sam. 12:7–9, 13)

---

*W. Ross Foley, *You Can Win Over Weariness*.

Therefore confess your sins to each other and pray for each other. (James 5:16)

$\mathcal{A}$nd don't think that basically we're really fine, that it's only around the edges that we still need a little polishing up. Don't say to the Lord or to anyone else, "Forgive the little thing or two I did. . . ." Little? Our sins are enormous! They put Jesus on that bloody cross!

The Publican pounded on his chest and cried, "Lord, be merciful to me, a sinner!" First John 1:9 tells us to confess our sins—but how can we confess them all? Part of our very sinfulness is that we're so dull, we don't understand much of our own sins. In the light of God's perfect standard of holiness, we are much worse than we think!

> Joseph de Maistre once said he did not know what a scoundrel's soul might be, but he knew well what the soul of a good man consisted of, and it was horrid. It is the whispered confession of us all.*

But God is so kind. When we "confess our sins"—whatever sins we *do* become aware of—He is "faithful and just, and will . . . purify us from *all* unrighteousness"! As you confess what you know, He will also forgive what you don't know. Partial confession produces total forgiveness. Praise the Lord!

> Jesus, Thy blood and righteousness
>   My beauty are, my glorious dress;
> Midst flaming worlds, in these arrayed,
>   With joy shall I lift up my head!†

Joanna: A Story of Renewal

---

*Ernest Dimnet, *The Art of Thinking*.

†Nicholaus L. Von Zinsendorf, 1700–1760; tr. John Wesley, 1703–1791.

*I*s the pace of your life too fast?

What is it that's driving you?

Is it perfectionism? That's pure ego. You'll self-destruct. Confess your perfectionism to God and ask Him for deliverance.

Is it desire for excellence "for the sake of your witness"? Whose excellence, yours or God's?

Is it pure social pressure? Maybe you need to say no to some activities that "everybody"—even Christians—are involved in. They're sapping more energy from you—or more finances— than you can afford to lose.

Is it love of money? This is so serious it's frightening. Jesus says you cannot serve both God and money (Matt. 6:24); you must choose one or the other. Wrestle that one to the ground and have done with it forever!

It will take the discipline of your heart to shift down.

Disciplines of the Heart

Give Him frequent spaces when you momentarily quit, relax, breathe deeply, stretch your body, and say, "Jesus, my eyes are on You. You are able. You are helping me from one moment to the next. I trust You."

As you release control to Him, He will make the hours stretch, bring others to help you, cancel some things you thought you had to do, show you duties you can delegate, show you duties that don't have to be done at all.

I didn't learn my lessons once for all. I've had to come back over and over to take seriously again His practical words,

> Reverence for God adds hours to each day.
> (Prov. 10:27 TLB)

Fix Your Eyes on Jesus

A work-centered life gets complex, and it leads to burnout. A Christ-centered life—even in the midst of work—stays basically simple, nourished and rested.

Then *don't fix your eyes on what you have to do.* When I've done that it's made me fragmented and harried.

"Martha, Martha," the Lord answered, "you are worried and upset about many things, but only one thing is needed. Mary has chosen what is better." (Luke 10:41–42)

Martha's problem wasn't cooking, it was the "many things." She was multi-directional, which always makes us oppressed, nervous, burdened, self-pitying, off-balance.

When your eyes are on Him, you begin to develop a reflex action inside you—it may take time—that shuns what's complicating, what's overwhelming. You'll find you want to *do less* (but do the most important things) to *become more.*

Although truly, the more you become, the more you actually achieve. And then your life begins to have wider-ranging and longer-lasting effects.

Fix your eyes on Jesus! Like Mary, focus; that's what I had to learn. Become a "one-thing" person (Luke 10:42).

Fix Your Eyes on Jesus

A friend of ours doesn't take one vacation a year, he takes hundreds, usually one or two hours long. He adds them to his lunchtime, or he tacks them onto drives to see clients, or he may take an early-morning one before he goes to the office.

He lightens his workload by building in brief respites along the way. Without quitting the journey, he refuels midflight.

Where does he go? What does he do? He explores. He prowls. He may visit a museum or an art gallery, or he may just open a door to see what's on the other side.

When we don't have time for any of those things we do this: We close our eyes for five to ten minutes and imagine we're at a favorite vacation spot. We imagine it as vividly as possible, with all the physical sensations that we'd notice if we were actually there: the sights, the sounds, the smells, the feeling of wind in our hair or sun on our skin . . .

After only a few minutes, our bodies begin to relax and respond as though we were actually there.

Or check this possibility: When you start for the shower, could you take a bath instead? A shower's quicker; but a bath could give you a mini-vacation. Besides, remember what the Japanese say, that no great thoughts are ever born in a shower!

Learn to take thousands of tiny vacations—just enough to get you refreshed for that next meeting, that next task—to maintain staying power for your work.

Keep refueling midflight.

You Don't Have to Quit

On the seventh day [God] rested. (Gen. 2:2)

$\mathcal{R}$ay and I were the speakers on a Caribbean cruise a while back, and on the cruise one day we ran into a lanky black crew member ankling down one of the ship's corridors, snapping his head back and waggling his elbows. "You gotta loose up!" he was chortling, "loose up!"

Hey, he was right! Resting in Christ *doctrinally* should "loose us up" *emotionally*. We won't be so tense! We won't get hurt so often. We'll laugh more.

Resting in Christ should "loose us up" *intellectually*. We can stretch to be less dogmatic on the fine points. Much as I hate to admit it, I'm probably not right nearly as often as I think I am! If we're rigid in our pet opinions, we're probably rigid in our muscles, too.

And speaking of that, resting in Christ should "loose us up" *physically*. We get so bloomin' serious over our foods and fear of foods, our exercises and fear of exercises, our medicines and fear of medicines, our sicknesses and fear of sicknesses.

Resting in Christ should "loose us up" *relationally*. We can be free to be ourselves and allow others the same privilege, receiving them as Christ receives us (Rom. 15:7).

And resting in Christ should "loose us up" *spiritually*. We may discover that what we thought was zeal for God was actually just a self-destructive intense personality.

Yes, of course we should "burn out for God"; I want to, too—to live all my life for Him. But we don't need to burn out for Him like gasoline—explosively, burning everybody around us in the process. We can burn out like charcoal—slowly, steadily, over a long period of time, and good to the last golden marshmallow!

Rest, my friend. "Make every effort to enter that rest" (Heb. 4:11). *Loose up.*

Disciplines of the Heart

34

*H*OW SINGLE, God, are You—how
        whole!
One Source are You, one Way, one Goal.
I tend to splinter all apart
With fractured mind, divided heart;
Oh, integrate my wand'ring maze
To one highway of love and praise.

O single, mast'ring Life of peace
At Whose command the ragings cease,
Keep calling to me "Peace, be still,"
To redirect my scattered will.
Keep gath'ring back my heart to You.
Keep cent'ring all I am and do.

O focused Spot of holy ground,
Silence which is the Source of sound,
I drop the clutter from my soul,
Reorganized by Your control;
Then single, whole, before Your throne,
I give myself to You alone.

—Anne Ortlund*

Disciplines of the Beautiful Woman

Where is the real you? It's deep inside of you, where your thinking and deciding really take place. Your life, as Ray says, is like a wheel, with the hub the true center of who you really are. The rim is all the places where your life touches this world, where there's apt to be plenty of friction, heat, and dust.

But in the center is the true you. If you have made God your highest priority of all, He is there. You are learning to abide in Him, and He in you. There is calm; there is peace. He is your refuge, to which you continually run. He is organization, and living in Him you sense control and plan. He is Spirit—your living and breathing, your laughter and tears—and all of it becomes holy because His Spirit is holy. Wonderful! Alleluia!

If God is at your life's center, then your mental and emotional life should reflect His presence, whether there's nobody around but you, or kids everywhere: "Whatever is true, . . . noble, . . . right, . . . pure, . . . lovely, . . . admirable [or attractive], think about such things" (Phil. 4:8).

And also, if this is true (that God is at your life's center) then your immediate surroundings ought also to reflect Him. Your immediate surroundings—your drawers and closets, your bedside table, your desk—are the filmiest clothing of your most personal, private life. Even if you have ten children, those areas should be yours alone, and they should reflect the order and peace of your inner life with God.

The smaller your family, the more the circumference of your immediate surroundings expands. If you're the unmarried president of a bank, you may have a whole penthouse to yourself. If you have many children, you may not have much of the house to call your own. If you share a college dorm room with two other girls, you have one-third of a room. Whatever is yours, let it reflect the beauty of a woman whose heart is with God.

Disciplines of the Beautiful Woman

> There is a way of ordering our mental life on more than one level at once. On one level we may be thinking, discussing, seeing, calculating, meeting all the demands of external affairs.
>
> But deep within, behind the scenes, at a profounder level, we may also be in prayer and adoration, song and worship, and a gentle receptiveness to divine breathings.*

*A*s you're reading this, breathe "alleluia," or whatever comes to mind. Just as you breathe air with your lungs—automatically and almost unconsciously—breathe Him with your spirit. "Glory to You, Lord." You hardly knew you said it.

It may be a quick request shot up—a quick telegram, almost wordless, but you and God both understand it. Notice Nehemiah 2:4: "The king said to me, 'What is it you want?' Then I prayed to the God of heaven, and I answered the king. . . ."

Pray always (Luke 18:1).
Pray continually (1 Thess. 5:17).
Pray on all occasions (Eph. 6:18).
> Where do you pray?
> In church (Ps. 111:1),
> in private (Matt. 6:6),
> in the open (on the beach, Acts 21:5;
> in a garden, (Luke 22:39–41),
> on your bed (Ps. 149:5)—
> everywhere (1 Tim. 2:8)!
"Pray in the Spirit on all occasions" (Eph. 6:18).

Disciplines of the Heart

---

*Thomas Kelly, *A Testament of Devotion*.

𝓗ow do you quit worrying? *You give up control.*

I can fuss and stew when I don't feel a sense of control over somebody or something. Then, again and again, I have to turn the control over to God—and immediately peace comes, and I rest.

Therapists tend to want to get you in control of a situation; that very need to control is the root of all paranoia. Give it up. Open your hands. Release it all to God. When you see your helplessness and ask God to help—only then is invisible machinery set in motion to start solving your problems.

Years ago Ginny and her eight-year-old Anna arrived as our new next-door neighbors. Ginny was in the process of divorcing, and she was panicky with fears that Scott would kidnap away their daughter. Only Psalm 91, repeated to Anna over and over every bedtime, restored Ginny's emotions enough for her to receive Christ as her Savior:

> I will say of the LORD, "He is my refuge and my
> fortress,
> my God, in whom I will trust." . . .
> He will cover you with his feathers,
> and under his wings you will find refuge. . . .
> You will not fear the terror of the night,
> nor the arrow that flies by day. . . .
> No harm will befall you,
> no disaster will come near your tent.

And it never did.

> Do not be anxious about anything, but in everything, by prayer and petition, with thanksgiving, present your requests to God. And the peace of God, which transcends all understanding, will guard your hearts and your minds in Christ Jesus. (Phil. 4:6–7)

Disciplines of the Home

It's not *your circumstances that shape you.* They are outside you and beyond you; they can't really touch you. *It's how you react to your circumstances that shapes you.* That's between your ears, and that affects the "real you."

And what controls your reactions? Abiding in Christ (John 15:4–10 KJV). Staying there.

Then what if you find, for instance, a lump in your breast? Of course you'll make a doctor's appointment immediately—but that's external. What happens within? *Lord, nothing important has changed. You love me. Your eternal, perfect plans for me are continuing on schedule. I will praise You; I will worship You. I will rest in all You're continuing to do in my life.*

Or what if you lose your job? You'll be your vigorous, efficient self in looking for another—if, indeed, He wants you to have another. But all that's external. What happens within? *The Lord is my Shepherd; I shall not want. I will fear no evil, for You are with me. My cup overflows. I praise You for this opportunity to praise You!*

Or what if you're confronted with any trauma at all? Psalm 112 is a wonderful psalm describing the godly person, and it says

> He will have no fear of bad news; his heart is steadfast, trusting in the LORD. His heart is secure, he will have no fear (vv. 7–8).

God's Word is God's Word! He's practical; He's realistic; He gives you every expectation of living on an even keel.

Disciplines of the Heart

The Old Testament calls Him a refuge, a fortress, a stronghold, a dwelling place. The New Testament says His name is Jesus Christ!

In the glorious terms of the New Testament gospel, you and I are *in Christ Jesus*.

> You're in Him the way a baby's in the womb—but better.
> You're in Him the way a future butterfly's in a cocoon—but better.
> You're in Him the way a deep-sea diver's in his diving suit—but better.
> You're in Him the way a bird's in the air or a fish is in the water—but better.

Being in Christ means you've been placed by God in a new environment—as James Stewart says, "transplanted into a new soil and a new climate—and both soil and climate are Christ."*

Confident in Christ

And being "in Christ" implies the meeting of all your life-needs. "My God will meet all your needs," says Philippians 4:19, " . . . in Christ." So no more discarding situations when they don't "meet your needs." You come to live at ease with imperfections because, behind the scenes, your deepest needs are being totally met—in Christ. You may change jobs or cities—but not because of unmet needs. Even a Colosseum with lions becomes possible—because *you know where you are—in Christ,* and you are drawing deeply from your Source.

> His divine power has given us everything we need for
> life and godliness through our knowledge of him who called
> us by his own glory and goodness. (2 Pet. 1:3)

Confident in Christ

---

*James Stewart, *A Man in Christ*

40

Once General Omar Bradley (so the story goes) was flying commerically and wearing civilian clothes. He hoped nobody would sit in the plane seat next to him because he had a lot of paperwork to do. But sure enough, someone sat down.

And not just anyone, but a very over-friendly, gum-chewing young Army private in uniform. Not having any idea who the general was, the young rookie said, "Hey, fella, if we're gonna fly together for two hours, we better get acquainted, right?" He stuck out his hand. "I'm Harry." "How do you do," said General Bradley.

"Lemme see, I'm gonna guess what you do. You look like a top salesman to me," the kid said. "No," said General Bradley.

"No? Big businessman?" "No," said General Bradley. "I'm in the same outfit you are, son. I'm in the Army."

"You gotta be a sergeant, then. Top sergeant?"

The general had had enough. "Young man, I am Omar Bradley, five-star general, and Chief of Staff of the Joint Chiefs of Staff of the armed forces of the United States of America."

"Izzat right, General?" The kid popped his gum. "You've got a big job. Don't mess it up!"

Respect for higher authorities, . . . for God!

Oh, it really is true that God invites us to "approach the throne of grace with confidence." But first we have to know that it's a throne of *grace*. We're not just to kick open the barroom door and bust in. When we see who we are, and who He is, we ought to get so trembling and weak-kneed that He has to *urge* us to come with confidence—"so that we may receive mercy and find grace to help us in our time of need" (Heb. 4:16).

For heaven's sake—yes, literally—our number-one life project must be to learn to "worship God *acceptably* with reverence and awe, for our 'God is a consuming fire'" (Heb. 12:28–29)!

Joanna: A Story of Renewal

41

Worship is not something we do as a luxury when we have the time in addition to other things we have to do. Worship is the very stuff of life, and while we are worshiping, God is working on our behalf and taking care of many things for us that we need to do—more than we could dream. And when we are busy and we worship, God is gently forcing us to live by faith, and to believe that He is making up the time!

Recently I read Daniel 4. The whole chapter is a remarkable testimony given by one of the most powerful emperors in world history, to tell how the only true God wouldn't let him go until he learned to worship Him!

Discipling One Another

And the Bible's final words tell us to adore and worship Him alone (Rev. 22:9).

Charles Spurgeon said,

> I hardly know how to describe adoration. Praise is a river flowing joyously in its own channel, banked up on either side that it may run toward its one object.
>
> But adoration is the same river overflowing its bank, flooding the soul and covering the entire nature with its great waters; and these not so much moving and stirring as standing still in profound repose, mirroring the glory which shines down up it, like summer's sea of glass; not seeking the divine presence, but conscious of it to an unutterable degree, and therefore full of awe and peace, like the Sea of Galilee when its waves felt the touch of the sacred feet. . . .
>
> It is the eloquent silence of the soul that is too full for language. . . .
>
> This should be the frequent state of the renewed mind.*

Joanna: A Story of Renewal

---

*Charles Haddon Spurgeon, *The Treasury of the New Testament,* vol. 3

ANNE'S NOTES ON ONE OF RAY'S SERMONS
"HOW TO WORSHIP WELL: EZEKIEL 44:9–16"

*A*doration: that yearning for God so deep that sometimes it's painful.

Easy for a Christian to work *for* God but not minister *to* Him. We can go through worship services to "get good feelings." Worship is a ministry to God Himself.

God has made us with energy, intelligence. If we don't spend them on God, we'll spend them on ourselves.

Ezekiel 44:10, 11, 13. Priests who had disobeyed could only minister *in the sanctuary*. Faithful sons of Zadok were allowed to minister *to the Lord* and come near to the most holy things (vv. 15–16). *We are qualified* (see Heb. 10:19–22)! Now we must do it.

Have an attitude of desire, of pressing in, ready to bless God. "One thing have I desired of the Lord." Not natural, supernatural.

When we come to worship we must meet God's needs first; then our own needs will be met!

Spurgeon, age twenty-two: "While the subject of God humbles the mind, it also expands it. The most excellent study for expanding the soul is the science of Christ and Him crucified, and the knowledge of the Godhead in the glorious Trinity. Nothing will so enlarge the intellect, nothing so magnify the whole of man."

Tozer: "God meant for a new convert to become a worshiper first. After that he can become a worker."

Up with Worship

43

*R*emember those great old words of George Fox: "It is a wonderful discovery to find that you are a temple, that you have a church inside of you, where God is. In hushed silence, attend to Him. The Lord is in His holy temple."

You're sitting in church: before the service, confusion or silent sterility; during the service, well-meaning but corny slapstick. Or coldness, polished to a high glaze. Or just grey, dreary sameness. Or whatever your particular church problem is.

So you don't care for the worship in your church? Well, it isn't the "worship" you're to worship; it isn't the minister or the music—it's God. Is He in your heart? Then apart from anything that's happening up front, out back, around you, anywhere— you can have your own private breakthrough into glory!

Oh, my friend, He waits to be all in all to you. He is sufficient. You and He in a worship service together? That's enough.

Think of all the places in the world where Christians can't meet in His name at all. Be humble, be grateful, be sweetened in your soul. A critical spirit won't bring the glory.

Does that mean be tolerant, be satisfied with the present state of things? No, no! Behind the scenes, agonize in prayer for that beloved church of yours.

But in church? Don't wait for "someday," and miss Him. You're there, He's there! Hooray! Three cheers for God! Sing! Pray! Celebrate! Let your face reflect the Presence!

Your personal worship doesn't depend on anybody else's behavior.

Up with Worship

*O*ne's ultimate loyalty must converge at a single point. To try to go two ways at once will rip a person down the middle."

> *(Vernard Eller)*

Jesus to Martha: "Only one thing is needed."
> *(Luke 10:42)*

"What is that one thing? Surely it is that God be loved and praised for Himself above all other occupations of the body or soul."

> *(The Cloud of Unknowing,*
> *fourteenth century)*

> . . . Thee will I cherish,
> Thee will I honor,
> Thou, my soul's glory, joy and crown!
>> *("Fairest Lord Jesus,"*
>> *seventeeth century)*

"The secret of successful Christians has been that they had a sweet madness for Jesus about them."

> *(A. W. Tozer)*

"As to other gods I am an atheist, but as to God the Son Who came forth from Him and taught us these things, I worship and adore Him."

> *(Justin Martyr, first century)*

> Glorious God,
> It is the flame of my life to worship thee,
>> the crown and glory of my soul to adore thee,
>> heavenly pleasure to approach.
>>> *(Old Puritan prayer)*

Fix Your Eyes on Jesus

*H*ave you subscribed to the world's values? Is *doing* more important to you than *being*? Then you're pressured.

Is *what you're acquiring* more important to you than *what you're becoming*? Then you're pressured.

Are jobs more important to you than relationships? Then you're pressured.

Do you think busyness, speed, and efficiency rank near the top of the list of virtues? Then you're pressured.

And are you ambitious to expose your children to more than most kids get? You're probably pressuring them.

Do you have huge expectations for them to achieve in many areas at once? You're pressuring them.

Do you want them to do, to be, marvelous extensions of yourself? You're pressuring them.

And, last, if you don't possess, deep in your soul, an assurance of God's acceptance of you and your family, and other people's acceptance of you and your family, then you're pressured and you're pressuring. Trying to justify yourselves, qualify yourselves, promote yourselves can take an awful lot of time.

Disciplines of the Home

> Do not love the world or anything in the world. If any-one loves the world, the love of the Father is not in him. For everything in the world—the cravings of sinful man, the lust of his eyes and the boasting of what he has and does—comes not from the Father but from the world. The world and its desires pass away, but the man who does the will of God lives forever. (1 John 2:15–17)

*L*isten to the quiet voice of love, with its sweet reasonableness, wanting the best for you (a "best" so good we can't imagine it):

> Come to me, all you who are weary and burdened, and
> I will give you rest. (Matt. 11:28)

"I have no desire," He says, "for you to go on being crushed under this great burden of trying to be what you're not and trying not to be what you are. Let it roll off. Let it go. What an enormous yoke it is! My dear, you're all exhausted from posing, from exaggerating, from hiding, from trying to *appear* instead of just *being*. Let Me help you take this ugly thing off. Poor child! Here, put on Mine instead:

> Take my yoke upon you and learn of me, for I am [meek] and
> humble in heart, and you will find rest for your souls. For my
> yoke is easy and my burden is light. (Matt. 11:29–30)

Says Christ, "My name is 'I AM WHO I AM,' as Exodus 3:14 puts it. "I don't try to defend Myself or to appear to be different than I am. Satan, on the other hand, 'masquerades as an angel of light' [2 Cor. 11:14], and all his followers try to do the same. It's part of their death struggle; they're on their way out.

"I never have had to do that," He continues, "and neither do My children. You are who you are: accepted in the Beloved, precious in My sight, and in the process of becoming perfect as I am perfect—a process so sure that I already see you that way!

"Isn't that enough? Aren't you satisfied with My plan?"

> Humble yourselves, therefore, under God's mighty hand,
> that he may lift you up in due time. (1 Pet. 5:6)

Disciplines of the Heart

Υou must hate what God hates and destroy what He wants destroyed. He knows the damage that enemies do to His children, the hurt and anguish they cause to His precious ones, and when He says "kill them"—*do it!*

Colossians 3:5–8 is this kind of command. God says,

> Put to death, therefore, whatever belongs to your earthly nature: sexual immorality, impurity, lust, evil desires and greed, which is idolatry. . . . Rid yourselves of all such things as these: anger, rage, malice, slander, and filthy language from your lips.

Look carefully at these things listed in Colossians 3, and ask yourself if you hate each one as God hates them. Do you let any of them hang around? Do you let them coexist in your life as if they were acceptable? Are you tolerating God's enemies?

Nehemiah didn't. When he came back from a trip and found Tobiah put up as a guest in God's house—Tobiah, who'd been God's enemy from the start—do you know what Nehemiah did? He literally threw out all Tobiah's stuff with his own two hands and had the room cleaned up and restored (Neh. 13:6–9).

Listen, the world is full of Christians who pass around little "spiritual" books and go to Bible classes and say "praise the Lord" a lot—at the same time showing no desire to put to death the characteristics of their earthly natures.

To people like these, the love of Jesus crucified is pure sentimentality. And whether they know it or not, they are utterly without power in their lives.

True Christianity costs.

Disciplines of the Heart

γou have failed in the past, and so have we. Do you feel disqualified? Do you feel as if you're already a "throwaway," that you "blew it" and you can't undo your mistakes? Does your record seem too blotted? Were your injuries too damaging, your mistakes too irreversible?

Friend, *your problem is no longer those past sins; your problem is how you're presently handling those sins.*

You have two choices.

1. You may choose chronic regret that leaves you defeated for the rest of your life. It could be an attempt at a do-it-yourself atonement; if you believe God doesn't easily forgive, then a way you can do something to help the process is by the penance of perpetual regret. That's a terrible misunderstanding of God. And it will do nothing but leave you unnecessarily shipwrecked.

2. Or you can choose "godly sorrow" over those past sins:

Godly sorrow brings repentance that leads to salvation and leaves no regret. (2 Cor. 7:10)

The father of the prodigal son put on a big party to honor his return. Now, the son wouldn't have made his father happier by sitting in a corner during the party mourning over his past. He honored his father by taking his word for it that all was really forgiven.

Regret over the sins of the past will haunt you until you truly believe how thoroughly God blots out your sins.

You Don't Have to Quit

Prayer:

"Lord, You have said that 'if we confess our sins, [You are] faithful and just and will forgive us our sins and purify us from all unrighteousness' (1 John 1:9).

"Lord, I do that right now."

> [Spend some leisurely time confessing to Him, in words, your sins.]

"O Lord, I realize how painfully incomplete this list is. You are so pure, I don't even begin to know all the multitude of ways that I offend a holy God.

"But, Lord, Your promise is that if I confess what I do know, You will purify me *from all unrighteousness*—everything I don't know as well—and make me wholly clean.

"How wonderful! Thank You, Father! What a blessing!

"And now, my God, I don't want to spend my life walking backwards, with my eyes always fixed on what I'm discarding.

> Forgetting what is behind, . . . I press on toward the goal.
> (Phil. 3:13–14)

"Lord, what a happy way to walk, with my face toward You! *I fix my eyes on Jesus.*

> The path of the just is like the shining light, that shineth more and more unto the perfect day. (Prov. 4:18 KJV)

"Alleluia!"

Fix Your Eyes on Jesus

I was sitting in the lounge of a Christian radio station, waiting my turn to go into the studio and guest a talk show. Another Christian program, on the air at that moment, was being intercommed into the lounge, so I couldn't help but listen. It was gross. In the name of "exposing" the sins of our day, shocking activities were being described, filthy words were being repeated.

I thought about all the New Testament letters, written and circulated in an equally obscene world; the Roman culture was then in its last throes of degradation. But the Scriptures didn't describe the society's filth, they only warned against it; and then spent the space teaching the positive—both in doctrinal truth and practical application for daily living.

Never does Paul say Christians "need to be informed" of what they're fighting against so they can "pray intelligently." No, no! He says, "Stay ignorant!"

> Be wise about what is good, and innocent about what is evil. (Rom. 16:19)

> It is shameful even to mention what the disobedient do in secret. (Eph. 5:12)

How do you become "blameless and pure, . . . in a crooked and depraved generation." (Phil. 2:15)?
Philippians 4:8 tells you how:
  Whatever is true,
  whatever is noble,
  whatever is right,
  whatever is pure,
  whatever is lovely,
  whatever is admirable—
  if anything is excellent or praiseworthy—
  think about such things.

Fix Your Eyes on Jesus

51

If any depression, any sadness, is longer than brief, it starts to become your very dangerous enemy.

Many people don't realize what a threat sadness is—and any danger which is unrecognized as a danger is all the more dangerous. There is no stigma against sadness. There is no embarrassment, no alarm, no rushing to the Lord to eliminate it.

But God's Word says,

The joy of the LORD is your strength. (Neh. 8:10)

And when a Christian is sad—whether he realizes it or not, *his power is diminished and he's vulnerable.*

A country that has internal unrest is the least able to resist any threatening foreign power. And a believer with sadness inside is the least able to resist any attack of Satan.

Depression is a sinister "fifth column" at work within the Christian community.

You watch a rejected congregation after a church split: As long as they're sad, there will be little true worship, little evangelism; the people can't focus away from themselves.

You watch an individual Christian who's sad: He's necessarily self-centered. As long as he's sad he—or she—makes a poor marriage partner.

When we're sad, we're sick. We don't function well. We don't lift and encourage other believers, and we don't appeal to unbelievers. Our spiritual strength and effectiveness are cut down.

No wonder the great George Mueller used to say, "It is my first business every morning to make sure that my heart is happy in God!"

Fix Your Eyes on Jesus

A fool gives vent to his anger. (Prov. 29:11)

*I*f you are angry at someone right now, you know the feeling in the pit of your stomach, and you know the words that race through your mind—words to tell that person and then words to tell others so they'll get on your side. . . .

Wait!

Wait. Cool down. Be quiet a minute. Think.

Look at Jesus. He "endured" (Heb. 12:2). He had every reason to be legitimately angry: Stupid, terrible people had unjustly done Him in—and yet He said,

"Father, forgive them, for they do not know what they are doing." (Luke 24:33–34)

You see, *the problem isn't really your troubler; it's within you.* All your life, sinners around you will sin—it's what they do best! But *fix your eyes on Jesus.* Remember His words:

Love is patient, love is kind. . . . [I]t is not easily angered, it keeps no record of wrongs. . . . It always protects, always trusts, always hopes, always perseveres. Love never fails. (1 Cor. 13: 4–8)

If anger is your problem, you may suddenly realize that Jesus' eye is fixed on you, studying you, and He asks you simply, "Doest thou well to be angry?" (Jon. 4:9 KJV). ("Is this improving you?")

Man's anger does not bring about the righteous life that God desires. (James 1:20)

Fix Your Eyes on Jesus

*L*ooking at your sin," wrote Theodore Monod, "only gives death; looking at Jesus gives life."

Psalm 32:3–4 and Psalm 38:3–10 both say that your personal sins, unrelieved by Jesus, can give you

> physical weakness,
> depression,
> heart palpitations,
> back pains,
> a tendency to infections,
> vision problems,
> and even bad posture.

Right now are you more aware of your sins than you are of Jesus? Focusing on them will do you in. There's no godliness in continually mourning over your sins. There's no merit in spending your life wringing your hands and crying, "I'm such a sinner! Oh, my awful sins!"

Any occupation with self is, in itself, sin. Then don't even make the matter of seeking to *renounce* your sins the big focus of your life.

If you're a man, do you play with toy cars? Probably not. You did as a boy—but there came a time when driving a real one was more fun, and you just quit playing with the others. You didn't give up toy cars; *they gave up you.*

If you're a woman, do you play with dolls? Probably not. You used to—but one day a fellow asked you out, and you discovered something better! You didn't give up dolls; *they gave up you.*

And when you fix your eyes on Jesus and you find out that He's flooding into you His resurrection life and power—you don't renounce a life of sin; *it will renounce you.*

Fix Your Eyes on Jesus

54

ℰphesians 6 is the classic chapter on what to do about Satan. How do you struggle against "the powers of this dark world and against the spiritual forces of evil in the heavenly realms"?

"Put on the full armor"—don't miss a single piece—of truth, righteousness, readiness that comes from the gospel, faith, salvation, and the Word of God; and through it all, praying always.

Put on every one of these:

1. *Salvation:* Make sure you're born again.

2. *The Word of God:* Get into a Bible class or a Bible correspondence course or some kind of instruction.

3. *Truth:* Learn right doctrine; expose yourself to Bible preaching, good radio teaching.

4. *Prayer:* It's not easy but crucial; keep a daily quiet time.

5. *Readiness that comes from the gospel:* Know what "the gospel," in a nutshell, really is—it's found, for instance, in 1 Corinthians 15:1–4—so you can share it.

6. *Righteousness:* Be careful to maintain moral integrity.

7. *Faith:* Trust yourself utterly to the Lord.

And notice something else: *Ephesians 6's solution is positive!* This armor against the devil is an aggressively happy, good lifestyle. *Simply seek to live a diligent Christian life.* That's the unsensational, steady, pleasant, poised, serene stance of power that will make the devil go bother somebody else.

> The prince of darkness grim,
> We tremble not for him!

Fix your eyes on Jesus—and Satan will probably stay far away.

Fix Your Eyes on Jesus

55

Blessed is he
    whose transgressions are forgiven,
    whose sins are covered.
Blessed is the man
    whose sin the Lord does not count against
        him
    and in whose spirit is no deceit. (Ps. 32:1–2)

Forgetting what is behind and straining toward what is ahead, I press on toward the goal. (Phil. 3:13–14)

*H*ave *you any idea the glorious life that could be yet ahead for you, if you take advantage of God's rehabilitation program?*

If regrets over the past have kept you from moving forward, understand that those very regrets need God's forgiveness, too. The negative memories, the wounds, the scars, the self-doubts—bring them all to the feet of Jesus and confess them as part of the whole mess of your sin. And—

If we confess our sins, he is faithful and just and will forgive us our sins and purify us from all unrighteousness. (1 John 1:9)

So don't cry over your past. For you it's halftime in the locker room, and the coach is saying, "Go on out. The game's not over yet."

You Don't Have to Quit

*W*hat is it God created you to do in your life?

He's had projects in mind for you since the beginning of time, which no one can complete but you. You are "God's workmanship, created in Christ Jesus to do good works, which God prepared in advance for [you] to do" (Eph. 2:10).

It's time for you to start fulfilling them.

Said the Lord to Jeremiah,

> "Before I formed you in the womb I knew you,
> before you were born I set you apart; . . .
> "Do not say, 'I am only a child.' You must go to everyone I send you to and say whatever I command you. Do not be afraid of them, for I am with you and will rescue you." (Jer. 1:5, 7–8)

And God has unique, specific plans just for you as well.

Then ask Him to show you what they are. That's not simplistic; that's utterly practical. He formed you to be His school teacher or His bank president or His janitor or His diplomat, for glorious, unique, strategic reasons.

You Don't Have to Quit

> Therefore do not be foolish, but understand what the Lord's will us. (Eph. 5:17)

*I*f you haven't before, deep inside your heart begin to believe a daring truth: God doesn't want you to live a mediocre life. In fact, here's His flat-out goal for you:

> That you may become blameless and pure, children of God without fault in a crooked and depraved generation, in which you shine like stars in the universe. (Phil. 2:15)

> That you may be able to discern what is best and may be pure and blameless until the day of Christ, filled with the fruit of righteousness. (Phil. 1:10–11)

You don't have to "live grey," feeling dirty, unworthy, mediocre, unfulfilled, and guilty.

And, my friend, whatever God asks you to be, He enables you to be! Second Peter 1:3 says that His divine power has given you *everything you need* for life and godliness! He says that you may even "participate in the divine nature and escape the corruption in the world caused by evil desires" (2 Pet. 1:4).

"How can such a thing be?" we ask in wonder, the way the Virgin Mary asked of the Christmas angel. And back from Colossians 2:9 comes the lofty magnificence of this bold statement of truth:

> In Christ all the fullness of the Deity lives in bodily form, and you have been given fullness in Christ[!]

Then how could you or I insult Him by living a cheap, grey, inconsequential life? He has promised that "He will be the sure foundation for your times, a rich store of salvation and wisdom and knowledge" (Isa. 33:6)!

Disciplines of the Heart

If you love God, take a look in Proverbs at *what He says your life is to be like*, reasonably and realistically:

> [You] will live in safety
>   and be at ease, without fear of harm. (1:33)

> When you lie down, you will not be afraid; . . .
>   your sleep will be sweet.
> [You will] have no fear of sudden disaster
>   or of the ruin that overtakes the wicked,
> for the LORD will be your confidence
>   and will keep your foot from being snared.
>   (3:24–26)

No shades of grey here!

Blessings will crown your head (10:6).
You'll point the way of life to others (10:17).
You'll be granted what you desire (10:24).
You'll stand firm forever (10:25)—you'll never be uprooted (10:30).
You'll win favor and a good name in the sight of God and man (3:4) . . . and on and on.

Does God lie, or does He even exaggerate? Then do you dare think this is all too good to be true?

Lift your eyes to the possibility that your life could really be *wonderful*.

Disciplines of the Heart

*P*ress on—and press on—and press on! Christian, there are so many in this world who are eager-beaver starters, and so few who are glorious finishers. The one thing I fear is that after I've encouraged other women toward Christ I'll stumble myself and fall on my face. I don't want to, oh, I really don't.

What am I learning in my life with Him? That Spirit-motivated *disciplines* facilitate the Christian walk. Oh, I'm not discounting all the warm feelings along the route, when I've sung Jesus-songs and held hands and the rest. But our sensuous age forgets that feelings come and feelings leave you, but the disciplines of life are what get you to where you want to go.

Do you feel as if your life is like a jammed closet, and you keep muttering now and then, "Someday I'm going to get organized"? Surrender yourself to Him afresh, right now, and ask Him what should be your first step of obedience.

Disciplines of the Beautiful Woman

We went to a seminar once where the speaker asked for smokers to raise their hands. One man raised his.

"But you're not a smoker," said the leader. "Yes, I am," answered the man.

"When did you last smoke?" the leader asked. "Just before the session," was the answer.

"Then," said the leader, "half an hour ago you were a smoker, but you're not at this moment. Now," he continued, "it's your choice, if you desire, to remain a nonsmoker for the rest of your life."

And we say to you, God is the God of new beginnings! "Now" is your fresh start. You are at this moment continuing to read this page, so *you are not a quitter*. And if you so desire, you can choose, one moment at a time from here on, to build into your life habits of commitment and staying power.

You Don't Have to Quit

*T*he "last days" are rushing upon us. God predicted how they would be—that the children would be disobedient to parents (2 Tim. 3:2)—eventually to the point of totally rebelling against them and having them put to death! (Matt. 10:21)

We're on the way. Families are falling apart. Divorce is a raging river. "Single adults" are multiplying—and so are sexual sins. More and more children are raised in confusion, and they're growing up to make second-generation messes. And in the rare homes still intact with both parents, there's often tension and yelling and noncommunication and too fast a pace.

Malachi said that either the hearts of the fathers must once again be turned toward the children, and the hearts of the children turned to the fathers—"or else [God] will come and strike the land with a curse" (Mal. 4:6).

The relationships between the generations must be healed, or else God's patience with us will run out.

Are your parents still living? Turn your heart toward them. Apologize to them for all your orneriness as a child (maybe even as a grown child. I was forty-six before I did that—and oh, it created such a warm, loving time for us!). If they're at a distance, phone, or at least write a letter. But hugs are best!

And right now, if you're a parent, turn your heart toward your children. If they're grown and away from you, they need an apology, by phone or letter. Knit your hearts closely, closely together.

Children Are Wet Cement

*H*alf a millennium ago a monk named Martin Luther re-discovered the meaning of *faith*. "The just shall live by faith!" he read, and raindrops of revival began to patter all around the world.

Then a century or more ago, believers rediscovered the meaning of *hope*. The Lord's return was the big news and the big study, and from it missions sprang to life, and study editions of the Bible, and Bible schools and Bible conferences and parachurch movements, and so on. More showers here and there!

In this generation believers are rediscovering the meaning of *love*. "Relational theology" is big. We are reaching for and finding each other. There are new longings for unity—organizational unity by some, but deeper than that. Denominational walls are breaking down. "Share" is the word. "Small group" is where the action is.

Faith has been rediscovered. *Hope* has been rediscovered. And now *love* is being rediscovered. But the greatest of these is love (1 Cor. 13:13)!

Discipling One Another

Can the Lord's return be far away?

[God's] mystery . . . for ages past was kept hidden in God, who created all things. His intent was that now, through the church, the manifold wisdom of God should be made known to the rulers and authorities in the heavenly realms, according to his eternal purpose. (Eph. 3:9–11)

> Look, he is coming with the clouds,
>   and every eye will see him,
> even those who pierced him;
>   and all peoples of the earth will mourn
>   because of him. (Rev. 1:7)

*W*hat a shock! At that moment millions will be begging, "*Wait!* Wait, I'm not ready!" But *time will have stopped.* And the Spirit will never again plead, "Today, if you hear his voice, do not harden your hearts" (Heb. 4:7)—*there'll be no more "today"!* Suddenly every person will be caught in his tracks. Like action on television, in an instant the frame will freeze! And then this verse will come true:

> Let him who does wrong continue to do wrong;
> Let him who is vile continue to be vile;
> Let him who does right continue to do right,
> And let him who is holy continue to be holy. (Rev. 22:11)

And it will be judgment time.

That's why 1 John 2:28 says, "Dear children, *continue* [or abide] *in him,* so that when he appears, we may be confident and unashamed before him at his coming."

Let's pray together: "O Lord God, we have all eternity to enjoy our rewards, and only a few short years to win them.

"Lord, *write eternity on my eyeballs.* May I see all things from Your perspective—and most of all, may I see You Yourself.

"O Lord, I want to live at this moment,
       and the rest of this day,
               and the rest of my life,
so that I can continually say, 'Come, Lord Jesus! Soon! Now!'"

Fix Your Eyes on Jesus

*B*ack before the world began, Christ shared the Father's glory (John 17:5), and with Him made all things (Col. 1:16).

God in Christ ordered the ground to fill up with seeds producing vegetation,

> the waters to fill up with fish,
>
>> the land to fill up with animals and insects. . . .

Then *God in Christ* commanded the plants and creatures to die,

> their bodies to fall back into the ground,
>
>> their remains to compress and become coal, diamonds, oil, gas—
>>
>>> vast, vast reserves of material, probably not all discovered even yet. . . .

Why?

All these lived not for themselves but for us. God in Christ was forming them long ago to heat winters they would never live through and light buildings they would never see.

God in Christ, with infinite wisdom and skill and love, was preparing a place for us. (The Ancient of Days, the Eternal One, loved us even back then.)

We've been destroying the place He prepared, by our sin. But Christ knew all along what we would do with this wonderful earth, His gift prepared with such love and skill—and He's getting a replacement ready: "Do not let your hearts be troubled. . . . In my Father's house are many rooms. . . . I am going there to prepare a place for you" (John 14:1–2)—*a second place for us in our resurrection, perfection, glory!*

If this first place was so beautiful and so equipped, what will the new one be? Jesus hasn't forgotten you; He has you in His heart. He's been getting another place ready, and He says, "I am making everything new" (Rev. 21:5)!

Fix your eyes on Jesus, and you'll stumble on wonder after wonder—and every wonder will be true.

Fix Your Eyes on Jesus

64

Christian, understand the nature of evil. Like any weed, it's alive, it's multiplying, it's maturing. It has its own dynamic; it tends not to wither but to grow toward full maturity. From one sin planted in Genesis chapter 3, came a huge harvest by chapter 6:

> The LORD saw how great man's wickedness on the earth had become, and that every inclination of the thoughts of his heart was only evil all the time. (6:5)

That's sin, for you. One seed can produce a terrible crop. It's true today, as well: evil is getting worse, it's maturing, it's on its way to its full bumper crop of the last days (2 Timothy 3).

But so is the wheat! "Satan is alive and well on planet earth"—but so is God! Don't get any fixation on Satan; don't let him become some kind of "reverse hero" in your eyes. Really, he's just a poor loser. And sin is actually stale, trite, dull.

On the other hand, think about the wheat. Righteousness doesn't seek to be noticed; it doesn't pay for many full-page ads; and yet its quiet influence is incredible.

"Jesus went about doing good"—and there was profound power in that. Goodness is dynamic, too! It's on the move; it, too, is growing toward its full bumper crop. Understand that sin is getting worse, but goodness is getting better.

Don't spend your time, then, clucking your tongue.

Celebrate righteousness! Celebrate God, who will win! As a Christian you're a victor!

Deeply believe that—in all your personal trials and in the worst of your family situations.

Your trust in God will color everything.

Disciplines of the Home

*P*erhaps this book you're reading has found its way behind iron or bamboo or other curtains. You say you live in a totalitarian state and you have little or no freedom? Hear the good news: In the only area where it really matters, you can be totally free. Between your ears, where you and God live together and interact and fellowship—where you're comforted and corrected and enjoyed by Him—you are utterly emancipated.

> And a light shined in the cell,
> > And there was not any wall,
> > And there was no dark at all,
> Only Thou, Immanuel.*

Disciplines of the Heart

> Strong are the walls around me
> That hold me all the day,
> But they who thus have bound me
> Cannot keep God away.
> My very prison walls are dear
> Because the God I love is here.
>
> They know, who thus oppress me
> 'Tis hard to be alone,
> But know not, One can bless me
> Who comes through bars and stone:
> He makes my dungeon's darkness bright
> And fills my bosom with delight.†

Fix Your Eyes on Jesus

---

*Amy Carmichael, "Light in the Cell," in *Toward Jerusalem*.

†Madame Jeanne Guyon (1648–1717), written when she was in solitary confinement, because of her Christian faith, in a prison in France.

*P*erhaps you say you're chained to an impossible husband. Think about Abigail; so was she. Nabal was rich but selfish and insensitive—a drunk and a bum, "surly and mean in his dealings" (1 Sam. 25:3).

And what was Abigail like? She was not just an escapist; she was realistic enough to call her husband a fool (v. 25). But she hadn't let him ruin her. When she talked to David, her speech revealed such a long-term, inner nurturing of godliness that her words came out almost like poetry:

> The life of my master will be bound securely in the bundle of living by the LORD your God. But the lives of your enemies he will hurl away as from the pocket of a sling. (1 Sam. 25:29)

Regardless of the crudeness around her, here was a woman of inner delicacy and sensitivity and beauty. Abigail's life was hidden in God. David recognized it immediately, and when God in His own time terminated Nabal's wretched life, David was quick to marry her. He knew a good thing when he saw it.

But Abigail didn't become lovely in the course of being David's wife: *She had already become lovely while she was the wife of Nabal.* Her real living was between her ears!

And, friend, as you stay close to God, so can your living be.

Disciplines of the Heart

*P*erhaps you say you're single and lonely; think about Ruth. She'd been widowed at an early age; she was childless; and she lived in a country far from her own home with a depressed mother-in-law (Ruth 1:20–21)! (Are things tough for you, as well?)

But Ruth lived in God. Whatever her external situation, she was happy, helpful, modest, sweet—everything God wanted her to be. She wasn't living from the outside in, letting her circumstances control her mood. She was living from the inside out. Her inner, constant connection with God gave her long-term perspective; how about you? Her real living was in secret, and her Father who saw in secret rewarded her openly: He gave her a wonderful second husband and made her an ancestor of Jesus Christ (Matt. 1:5).

Disicplines of the Heart

Let us fix our eyes on Jesus . . .
>>that He may cast us down, and that He may
>>>raise us up;
>>that He may afflict us, and that He may
>>>comfort us;
>>that He may despoil us, and that He may
>>>enrich us;
>>that He may teach us to pray, and that He
>>>may answer our prayers;
>>that while leaving us in the world, He may
>>>separate us from it,
>>>our life being hidden with Him in God,
>>>and our behaviour bearing witness to Him
>>>>before men.*

Fix Your Eyes on Jesus

---

*Theodore Monod, early twentieth century

*P*erhaps you say it's too late; you're getting old, and your whole life has been terrible; think about Miriam.

As a little girl, one of millions of captive Jews cruelly oppressed in Egypt, Miriam's parents had hidden her tiny brother, Moses, and made her responsible for protecting him. Unfortunately he got confiscated, which permanently split up the family. Did Miriam deeply grieve, thinking this was all her fault?

Not until Miriam was in her upper eighties did something good finally happen to her! Was it too late to take advantage of it? Here were her two younger brothers, who had survived their ordeals but were now aged eighty-three and eighty, finally leading all the Hebrews out of the land.

Do you think Miriam complained about leaving her home or about the length of the walk? Listen, as soon as the opportunity for leadership emerged, she was right there. And when everybody started singing the great song Moses had made up about the escape,

> Miriam . . . took a tambourine in her hand, and all the women followed her, with tambourines and dancing. Miriam sang to them:
>
>> Sing to the LORD,
>>> for he is highly exalted.
>> The horse and its rider
>>> he has hurled into the sea. (Exod. 15:20–21)

Her choice was in the disciplines of her heart: to be just one more little old woman in the world, or to rise to fulfill God's great plans for her life. She chose the latter, and for the next forty years she joined her two brothers in leadership! My friend, your future, too, is full of promise! God ordains that the best wine will be last (John 2:10)!

Disciplines of the Heart

*P*erhaps you say your problem is different from most others': You're raising your children in a godless community full of pressures toward immorality—so you have a right to stew, not for yourself but for your children.

Think about Mordecai—a man, it's true, but a substitute mother. Mordecai was one of thousands of captured Jews in Persia, where the culture was so pagan and oppressive that if the name "God" had appeared in the book of Esther that tells his story, the book wouldn't have survived for us to read.

Mordecai had assumed the responsibility for raising his little orphaned niece, Esther—and this in a situation where neither he nor she had any personal freedoms whatsoever. So when King Xerxes was looking for a new queen, neither of them could object when Esther was taken and put into the harem of girls being tried out for the king!

How would you feel?

Well, Mordecai had parented his little niece as best he could, and both of them were in the capable hands of Almighty God. So when Esther was away from Mordecai's influence and even in impossible circumstances, God gave her courage, and she saved her entire captive people from on-the-spot extermination. Mordecai's faith and Mordecai's faithfulness were both rewarded.

How big is your God?

Disciplines of the Heart

70

$\mathcal{A}$re you right now in a financial crunch? Maybe God has created the shortfall to teach you dependence and prayer. What's He saying to you? What are you learning? . . . Keep your attention on the divine Distributor.

> The eyes of all look to you,
>> and you give them their food at the proper
>>> time.
> You open your hand
>> and satisfy the desires of every living thing.
>>> (Ps. 145:15–16)

Never, never does He mean for you to exhaust yourself "like the heathen" (Matt. 6:32)—like all those orphans!

Yuppies hyperaggressive to "be millionaires by thirty" are doing to themselves physiologically exactly what Columbia River salmon do, fighting their way upstream. The salmon, also, are "climbing the ladder," and they make it—and then die of cardiovascular exhaustion. Learning to be content (see Psalm 131) will literally heal your heart.

> It is senseless for you to work so hard from early morning until late at night, fearing you will starve to death; for God wants his loved ones to get their proper rest. (Ps. 127:5 TLB)

> He gives food to those who trust him; he never forgets his promises. (Ps. 111:5 TLB)

Ask Him, because He's trying to teach you to pray. But also *expect Him* to take care of you. If you truly believe that the Lord is your Shepherd, then you shall not want.

Disciplines of the Home

Get drastic new wisdom for spending your money.

The spirit of the world is discontent and greed. I'm all for free enterprise—but the fact is, the free enterprise system, over-used, can keep you so dissatisfied that you buy and buy and buy.

Now, there's nothing basically wrong with living comfortably and dressing well and driving a nice car. It depends on the price! If they came at the cost of too much debt, or disagreeing over whether to buy or not to buy, or simply out of spirit of discontent; or if desire for them makes us cut back on saving or giving, or makes us take on too many jobs to pay for them—then, for us at this time, they're wrong.

> Keep your lives free from the love of money and be content with what you have. (Heb. 13:5)

As parents, as a family, *discipline your desires.*

Otherwise, four things will happen: 1. Your family life will have an atmosphere of being cheated, or being incomplete. 2. You'll place unbearable strain on your marriage. If either spouse is pressured by the other to supply more than he or she can supply, there will be a deep sense of inadequacy and failure. 3. You'll compound stress in your children. "An environment, where the best is always in the future," says Tim Kimmel, "breeds an attitude that makes the present look cheap."* 4. You will play into the hands of the powers of this world system that want to control you. Your chronic borrowing from them to "keep up" makes you their servant and makes them your lords. "The rich rule over the poor, and the borrower is servant to the lender" (Prov. 22:7).

Disciplines of the Home

---

*From Tim Kimmel's *Little House on the Freeway* as quoted in *Focus on the Family Magazine*, February 1988.

1. *God creates and owns all money and all material things.* He says, "I have no need of your gifts to Me. I own everything." "If I were hungry I would not tell you, for the world is mine, and all that is in it." (See Ps. 50:9–12.)

2. *God distributes money and material things as He chooses.* Humans and all living things are absolutely dependent on His distribution. "These all look to [God] to give them their food at the proper time" (Ps. 104:27).

3. *God knows that in the human heart, money is His great rival*—that it's either/or. "You cannot serve both God and Money" (Matt. 6:24). "Some people, eager for money, have wandered from the faith" (1 Tim. 6:10).

4. *One of God's clearest promises is to keep His children supplied.* "My God will meet all your needs according to his glorious riches in Christ Jesus" (Phil. 4:19). (And see Ps. 37:25.)

5. *God tests your faith by asking you to give to Him first, before you receive His supply.* "Seek first his kingdom and his righteousness, and all these [material] things will be given to you as well" (Matt. 6:33). "Give, and it will be given to you" (Luke 6:38).

Money is a powerful way God seeks to build into your life two qualities: compassion and faith.

Building a Great Marriage

Now, brothers, we want you to know about the grace that God has given the Macedonian churches. Out of the most severe trial, their overflowing joy and their extreme poverty welled up in rich generosity. For I testify that they gave as much as they were able, and even beyond their ability. . . . And they did not do as we expected, but they gave themselves first to the Lord (2 Cor. 8:1–3, 5).

*H*ere's a nineteenth-century person riding along in his carriage on a dark but star-lit night.

He's got all his coach lights on, so as he drives along he can see in front of him just fine. But with those strong lights all around him he can't very well see the stars—just the way, if you're a materialist, you can't very well see Jesus.

Now, says Kierkegaard, on this dark but star-lit night here comes a poor peasant. He has no carriage and no lights at all, so you'd think he'd get a glorious view of the stars. The only problem is, he's probably so busy looking down to make sure he doesn't fall in a hole, he doesn't see the stars, either.

And if you get rid of every single material possession—just the business of living would certainly be more awkward, and probably be so distracting and consuming that you wouldn't fix your eyes on Jesus, either: Asceticism is no answer.

So the big question is: How many lanterns do you need? How many material things are just the right amount, to live efficiently enough and yet still have a good sight of Jesus?

"These things can be good—*very* good—*if they are used to support man's relationship to God rather than compete with it.*"*

Nobody can tell you how many lanterns you personally need, and don't judge anyone else's decisions. The only point is, keep your own lanterns few enough so that most of all, you can see Him!

> Turn your eyes upon Jesus, Look full in His
> wonderful face,
> And the things of earth will grow strangely dim,
> In the light of His glory and grace.†

> *Fix Your Eyes on Jesus*

---

*Vernard Eller, *The Simple Life*.

†Copyright 1922; renewed 1950 by H. H. Lemmel. Assigned to Singspiration, Inc.

$\mathcal{M}$y brother Bobby and I used to play marbles on our living-room rug. He always won, but I was a sucker and we'd keep playing until Mother called us to dinner.

We never thought to ask each other, "Do you think we'll get any dinner tonight? Do you think Daddy brought home any food? Do you think Mother cooked it? What if they've forgotten us? What if they've decided not to feed us any more? Should we have done something to earn it, so they'd keep giving it to us?"

Hey, we were their kids. Our job was to play marbles, and their job was to supply the grub!

If you get momentarily anxious over finances, picture yourself a little kid playing on the floor. Your job is basically just to wait for the dinner call. This is not to say you shouldn't work and have a sense of responsibility (2 Thess. 3:6–13), but *your source of supply is not your paycheck from your work.* Your source of supply is your heavenly Father, who knows better than you do what you need (Matt. 6:32) and has promised to supply just the right amount.

Disciplines of the Heart

All things are yours;
All are yours,
and you are of Christ,
and Christ is of God.
(1 Cor. 3:21–23)

When you see that Christ is everything,
and you make Him your everything,
then you have everything.

Fix Your Eyes on Jesus

75

*T*he apostle Paul begins his letter to the Colossians—and to you—with such tender and exciting words! He says,

> To the holy and faithful brothers in Christ at Colosse: Grace and peace to you from God our Father. (Col. 1:2)

"What?" you say. "I'm neither holy nor faithful. I fight bad thoughts, I sense a lot of ego in me, I lose my temper, I'm weak, I want my own way."

Remember the difference between your standing and your state! God sees not your state but your perfect standing in Christ—and in His eyes you *are* "holy and faithful."

But there's more; let's dig deeper. Even looking at your present state, which seems to you shaky and inconsistent, God says you are very special. Like a compassionate parent who mercifully reads into his child the best, and who affirms his child ahead of time to gently nudge him to *become all he needs to become,* so God says to you, "My dear child, you are Mine, and you are already loved, cherished, and special. I have chosen you out of the world to be separate, different, set apart, to become like Me. My love and My promises right now rest upon you.

"Don't argue with Me. Don't fight what I'm saying. I see you now as you will be through all eternity. I consider you holy and faithful."

If that's truly how God sees you, then you stand taller, don't you, and you *want to become* holy and faithful, in order to measure up to His generous assessment!

Confident in Christ

$\mathcal{R}$ecently the New York City Police Department investigated a tragic death. Sprawled in a filthy back alley lay an old "bag lady" who had finally lost her battle with life. For years she'd kept her body going by stealing the leftovers off plates in restaurants—but the more efficient the restaurants became, the more those food scraps were denied her. At last her frail, dirty shell gave up.

Then the newspapers revealed the news: Investigations showed she'd had many bank accounts, each holding hundreds of thousands of dollars! This old woman's *standing* was with the wealthy of the city, but her *state* was that of a miserable pauper.

Christian, do you ever live spiritually as if you were poor? Do you get discouraged, do you worry, as if you had no resources—when God has given you everything in Christ? The world is full of spiritual "bag ladies" whose *states* are tragically inconsistent with their *standings*.

Oh, that you would take comfort in Hebrews 10:14: "By one sacrifice [Christ] has made perfect forever those who are being made holy."

There! Do you see it?

"Made perfect forever." You're already perfect: That's your *standing*.

"Being made holy." You are, during your walk with Christ, being made holy: That's your *state*.

And both are simultaneously true.

Hold up your head, Christian; take a deep breath and let God encourage you!

Being confident of this, that he who began a good work in you will carry it on to completion until the day of Christ Jesus. (Phil. 1:6)

Confident in Christ

*I*t's one thing to be a saint; that's your *standing*. It's another thing to be saintly; that's your *state*. God's part of the deal is perfect, but our part isn't.

Colossians 3:1–5 spells out the difference:

> Since, then, you have been raised with Christ [that's your standing],
> Set your hearts on things above [make your present state consistent with such a standing].
> Set your minds on things above, not on earthly things. [Discipline your state to be worthy of your standing.]

Here's your standing:

> For you died, and your life is now hidden with Christ in God. When Christ, who is your life, appears, then you also will appear with him in glory.

So let your state be this:

> Put to death, therefore, whatever belongs to your earthly nature: sexual immorality, impurity, lust, evil desires and greed, which is idolatry.

Who wouldn't want to, when God has given us such a standing? How embarrassing to us, how disappointing to Him, to live as if we were still in our old life, when we realize the way He chooses to see us!

Confident in Christ

Your standing in Christ is not progressive.

Let's take a six-year-old child who trusts in Jesus. His understanding of the faith will grow, of course; but that child is no less "accepted in the Beloved" than Christians who've walked with the Lord sixty years. You're accepted by the virtue of Christ, not because of your longevity.

Or take an adult who's known the Lord for only a month. He's no less a Christian than an old timer. His sins are just as forgiven; his destination is just as sure.

Ephesians 1:5 says that every Christian is adopted into full sonship. Two meanings for *adopted* are possible: One is the way we understand it today; the other was a Roman custom similar to being "Bar Mitzvahed." Up to a certain age the child was considered a minor member of the family—loved and cared for, but without much status or responsibility. He was trained and schooled and disciplined and held under until the day of his adoption, the day when the father decided he was mature enough to be considered an adult son (see Gal. 4:1–2). At this point, with great celebration, he was "adopted"; he became a full heir to all the father's holdings and accepted as a man in the family.

How different from that when you came into Christ! At the moment you were born into God's family you were adopted without any probationary period at all! Immediately He gave you—spiritually a newborn babe—the full privileges of adult sonship. Amazing!

That is why we say your "standing" is not a condition into which you progress; it's a position in which you're placed. It can't be improved on.

Confident in Christ

For you did not receive a spirit that makes you a slave again to fear, but you received the Spirit of sonship. And by him we cry, "*Abba*, Father." (Rom. 8:15)

79

*R*ecently we saw a foreign family huddled on the sidewalk at the Orange County airport—obviously new refugees from somewhere in Southeast Asia. They looked so frightened and confused! Around them were a few sacks of possessions, and they seemed very much alone.

Soon all of us were relieved to spy a couple who were apparently this family's sponsors. An interpreter was along, explanations were made, and soon they all went off together. What a wonderful thing to think that here was another needy family in the world being tenderly received into a new country, given a place to stay, provision made for their needs, and given a fresh start in life! We commented to each other that it would take months, perhaps years, for that family to discover all the great advantages that were suddenly theirs as new residents of America.

Did you know that from the moment you believed in God's Good News, you were transported from the kingdom of darkness to the kingdom of light? At that moment God placed you into Christ—and it will take eternity for you to understand all the fabulous advantages of your new position in Him.

Confident in Christ

Praise be to the God and Father of our Lord Jesus Christ, who has blessed us in the heavenly realms with every spiritual blessing in Christ. (Eph. 1:3)

$\mathcal{D}$ay by day, morning by morning, begin your walk with Him in the calm trust that *God is at work in everything.* George Mueller used to say, "It is my first business every morning to make sure that my heart is happy in God." He was right! It is your personal business, as a discipline of your heart, to learn to be peaceful and safe in God in every situation.

Some of my mornings I read this, written in my notebook:

> The light of God surrounds me;
> The love of God enfolds me;
> The power of God protects me;
> The presence of God watches over me;
> Wherever I am, God is.

Remember, friend, where your real living is going on. In your thinking, in your reacting, in your heart of hearts—here is where your walk with God begins and continues. So when you start to move into trusting Him, *stay there.* Don't wander out again into worry and doubt!

Disciplines of the Heart

It is very pleasant to live here in our beautiful world. My eyes cannot see the beautiful things, but my mind can see them all, and so I am joyful all the day.

—*So said blind and deaf Helen Keller*

Fix Your Eyes on Jesus

81

God is at work in everything.

Do you believe that? You won't truly rest and trust if you believe He's only at work in some areas of your life, and the remainder is up to you. Then you'll come out hassled and tired.

Don't think God is at work in some activities but not in others. Sometimes I've heard Christians pray when they come to a church meeting or a retreat, "Lord, it's so good to come back to You out of the bustle and stress. . . ." I want to interrupt, "He's been with you all the time! How tragic if you've been living until now as if you were on your own!"

Don't think God is at work on Sundays but not from Monday to Saturday. Don't think God is at work in healings but not in sicknesses. Don't think God is at work in good times but not in bad.

Have you noticed Jonah's ups and downs (or should I say ins and outs)?

"The LORD provided a great fish" (Jon. 1:17) to rescue him from drowning.

"The LORD provided a vine" (4:6) to shade him.

Then "God provided a worm" (4:7) to destroy the shade.

And then "God provided a scorching east wind" (4:8).

The Lord provided them all: two goods, two bads.

Or think about Joseph; "the Lord was with him" in great times or in terrible times:

His master saw that *the LORD was with him* and that the LORD gave him success in everything he did. (Gen. 39:3)

While Joseph was there in prison, *the LORD was with him.* (vv. 20–21)

You have that sweeping statement in Romans 8:28 that says flatly that God is at work in everything for you: "We know that in all things God works for the good of those who love him."

Disciplines of the Heart

What a release, what a freedom indeed, to be delivered from trying to manage my own Christian life and to let Him take over! "The [person who] has discovered this secret of simple faith has found the key that will unlock the whole treasure-house of God!"*

I love J. B. Phillips's picture of this life in his translation of Romans 5:17: "Men by their acceptance of his . . . grace and righteousness should live all their lives like kings"!

Comments Oswald Sanders,

> What a fascinating picture of Christian living this vivid picture portrays: nobility, charm, authority, wealth, freedom. Our God invites us to believe that these spiritual qualities and prerogatives may and should be enjoyed by every child of the King of Kings. If we do not manifest and enjoy them, it is not because they are beyond our reach, but only because we are living below our privileges.†

I stop writing and sit a little taller. My heart shouts *halleluia!* As you read, are you joining me? Let's tell Him we never again want to live below our privileges—not when He has gone to such lengths to provide them, and not when He so delights in our receiving them!

Disciplines of the Heart

> Blessed assurance, Jesus is mine!
>   Oh, what a foretaste of glory divine! . . .
> This is my story, this is my song,
>   Praising my Saviour all the day long.
>   —Fanny J. Crosby

---

*Hannah Whitall Smith, *The Christian's Secret of a Happy Life*.
†Oswald Sanders, *Spiritual Maturity*.

*D*o you know that your groveling before God makes Him impatient? Making ourselves nothing in order to make Him everything really turns Him off. (Ray and I understand that; I can't abide for him to put himself down, and neither can he stand it when I belittle myself. That's the way lovers are.)

It *is* our place to remember what we are, in ourselves, in order to appreciate all that we are in Christ! But self-occupation (whether we're saying "I'm wonderful" or "I'm a louse") is sin, and God won't have it.

When Moses demeaned himself (Exod. 4:10), God's anger "burned against" him (4:14). He can't stand to have His cherished children reviled by others or even by themselves.

You stumble to the door of a castle—ragged, filthy, embarrassed, insecure. . . .

And when you go in, the King Himself eagerly takes over. He welcomes you with all His heart, bathes and clothes you gorgeously, and makes you the guest of honor at a royal feast.

But *you must receive it all.* Don't you dare sit in a corner miserable because you're remembering who you are and where you came from. That wouldn't honor your Host! He loves you, and He did it all to give you the time of your life.

And *you must stay there.* Well, who would be so rude—or so foolish—as to leave?

The king has brought you into his chambers. (Song of Sol. 1:4)

The friends are standing around rejoicing and delighting in you.

Relax! Enjoy! Forever!

Disciplines of the Heart

𝒴ou are in Christ, who is the glorious Total of God. Spiritual "poor talk" is out. "I'm not much," "I can't do that," "I don't have enough resources," "Who am I . . . ?" are all inappropriate for a child of the King. Without Him you are nothing; but in Him you are rich, able, full, complete.

When Christ lived on earth He was the visible display of the triune God. The word *fullness* or *completeness* means that Jesus Christ was Deity running over. Colossians 1:19 says, "For God was pleased to have all his fullness dwell in him."

Who can explain God? It takes all of Jesus Christ to explain Him. There are hundreds of functions and facets and names of Jesus: the Light, the Ancient of Days, the I AM, Wonderful Counselor, the Light of Israel, the Branch, the Rock, the Lord, the chief Cornerstone, the Way, the Truth, the Life, and on and on. He is the express image of God's Person, but it takes every facet of Him to reveal fully the glories of the Godhead.

This is the Christ in whom you've been placed. This is the Christ who surrounds you—above you, beneath you, around you, before you, behind you, within you. This is the Christ who is all, and in all. You are complete, "running over," in Him!

As He is now in heaven, so are you in this world. You are in His name, in His plans, in His power, in His dignity, in His authority, in His reign, in His grace. When you come to Him by faith, all this and more comes to you.

In Christ you are in that vital, dynamic, eternal environment of the power of glory. Colossians 2:7 says you are in Him as a plant is in soil—living, rooted, growing, flourishing, and drawing all from Him.

Confident in Christ

*I*f you've ever been the victim of an action that's blatantly unfair, consider Jesus. Acquitted by the highest court of the land ("I find no basis for a charge against him," John 19:4–6), He is led away and roughly nailed to a cross to die anyway!

Even in this crisis, the habit of His life continues: He prays. "Father, forgive them. . . ."

Who is "them"?

Not just the Italian soldiers carrying out the act.

Not just the Jewish mob shouting, "Let his blood be on us and on our children!"

Father, forgive all people from Adam on: "all have sinned." All are responsible for His death.

Forgive *me*, Anne Ortlund.

Forgive *you*, reader.

". . . *For they do not know what they are doing.*"

You didn't know; I didn't know—we weren't even born yet!

Remember the Old Testament Israelites who qualified to live in one of the Cities of Refuge because they'd accidentally killed somebody? We're like that. We crucified Jesus "unintentionally and without malice aforethought" (Josh. 20:5).

Nevertheless, we did it: We killed Him. We sinned—and to pay for us, He had to die.

Wrote Johann Heerman in about 1630—and he was right—

> Who was the guilty? Who brought this upon
>   Thee?
> Alas, my treason, Jesus, hath undone Thee!
> 'Twas I, Lord Jesus, I it was denied Thee:
> I crucified Thee.

Fix Your Eyes on Jesus

*A*nd *it was so terrible, when it happened all nature went bonkers.*

From high noon to mid-afternoon, a thick blanket of darkness covered everything.

An earthquake rattled the land so violently that rocks split.

Tombs broke open, and people long dead got up and walked out of their graves and into the city!

The walls of the temple were left undamaged—and yet inside, the great thirty-by-sixty-foot curtain separating the Holy Place (where priests could go) from the Most Holy Place (where dwelt the presence of God) was split right down the middle—interestingly, from the top to the bottom.

"Surely this man was the Son of God!" said one soldier (Mark 15:9). There was no other explanation. And yet—

> The scandal of the incarnation . . . [is] the shame of a God Who has so wallowed in the muck and misery of the world that He has become indistinguishable from it.*

> When we shall see him, there is no beauty that we should desire him.
>
> He is despised and rejected of men, a man of sorrows, and acquainted with grief: and we hid as it were our faces from him; he was despised, and we esteemed him not. (Isa. 53:2–3 KJV)

Fix Your Eyes on Jesus

---

*Frederick Buechner, *The Faces of Jesus.*

87

$\mathcal{S}$urely you are not another of this man's disciples?" the girl at the door asked Peter.

He replied, "I am not." . . .

Then Pilate took Jesus and had him flogged. The soldiers twisted together a crown of thorns and put it on his head. They clothed him in a purple robe and went up to him again and again, saying, "Hail, king of the Jews!" . . .

They crucified him. (John 18:17; 19:1–3, 18)

O CHRIST, the crown of death was on Thy
            brow,
And in Thine eyes deep mystery and pain;
The Kingdom seemed forgotten then—but now,
        Lord, take Thy crown and reign!

O Christ, with what derision did they bow
And mock Thee, stripped of robings and of
            throne;
And hatred seemed to win the day—but now,
        Lord, reign, and reign alone!

O Jesus, when I think of Peter's vow,
I wonder: might I curse Thee and depart?
Hold fast my consecration here and now;
        Lord, reign within my heart!

—Anne Ortlund

Women's Devotional Bible

*J*esus knew . . . that he had come from God and was returning to God; so he got up from the meal, . . . poured
water into a basin and began to wash his disciples' feet. (John
13:3–5)

Christ Jesus, . . . being in the very nature of
                    God, . . .
made himself nothing,
       taking the very nature of a servant. (Phil. 2:5–7)

Lord, I'm amazed at Your heavenly Son:
You gave Him honor when the world begun,
You sat Him in glory on the Mercy Seat—
But He got right down and washed disciples'
              feet!

Lord, I'm amazed at Your heavenly Son:
He rose from table when the meal was done,
Put water in a bowl, as a servant would,
For He wanted His disciples clean and good.

Lord, I'm amazed! Your Begotten One
He shone in heaven like a mighty sun!—
But when He looked down upon my tear-
              stained soul,
Then He knelt down to earth and washed me
              whole!

Think of it, Lord! You gave Him seas and sands,
       And there He was with a towel in His hands!
Think of it, Lord! You gave Him sands and seas,
       And there He was, down on His knees!*
                         —*Anne Ortlund*

                  Discipling One Another

89

By Thy sweat bloody and clotted! Thy soul in
        agony,
Thy head crowned with thorns, bruised with
        staves,
Thy pierced hands and feet,
Thy strong cry, Eli, Eli,
Thy heart pierced with the spear,
The water and blood thence flowing,
Thy body broken, Thy blood poured out—
Lord forgive the iniquity of Thy servant
And cover all his sin.*

*T*he Lancelot Andrewes quotation above was to end this chapter. But when I'd written these words I got down on my face on the floor.

I groaned, "O God, O God! Have I written this chapter hoping I've written 'powerfully' to touch people about Your crucifixion—so they'd buy the book and I'd make money? Am I standing near the cross hawking my wares to take advantage of the Great Event?

"Then I'm another Demetrius!" (You remember him, the silversmith. He lived under the shadow of the great goddess idol Artemis, and he didn't want Christ preached because he made a good income selling little silver shrines to the tourists who came to worship her.)

Oh, a thousand, thousand curses on all Demetriuses!

I, too, bow myself at Jesus' cross, in humility and shame. I repent of all my personal sin that put Him there.

You do the same.

O Lord, Lord! Forgive us our dry eyes.

Fix Your Eyes on Jesus

---

*Lancelot Andrewes, quoted by Oswald Sanders in *Christ Incomparable*.

Jesus' resurrection makes all the difference in your personal life. That's where everything changes!

He offers you His presence.

In His earthly body Jesus could only be in one place at one time (Lk. 10:1). But in His resurrection body—"On the evening of that first day of the week, when the disciples were together with the doors locked for fear of the Jews, Jesus came and stood among them" (John 20:19).

When I'm finished speaking somewhere I can easily worry, "Did I come across too bossy, did I come across too unfeeling and hard-nosed, did I put anybody down, did I offend, did I intimidate, did I act like the big know-it-all," and so on, and so on—and I agonize. *My eyes are on myself.*

But because our Jesus is risen and omnipresent, I can say, "Refocus my eyes on You, Lord. I committed this all to You before I began. I believe You took charge, and that You covered all my humanness that would have distracted from You." And I put that session in my two hands and surrender it to Him again.

And *He is near* (Phil. 4:5), and He comforts me.

At His birth He was given two names, "Jesus" (Matt. 1:21) and "Immanuel" (Matt. 1: 23). "Jesus" means "Saviour," and He was called that all His earthly life.

But "Immanuel" means "God with us," and it's more appropriate now than ever.

He is with you right now, as you read this. Fix your eyes on Him.

> The light of Christ surrounds you.
> The love of Christ enfolds you.
> The power of Christ protects you.
> The presence of Christ watches over you.
> > Wherever you are, Christ is.

Fix Your Eyes on Jesus

Because of His resurrection He offers you His peace. Said the newly risen Christ, "Peace be with you!" (John 20:19–20).

"Shalom," the Hebrew word for it, means wholeness, health, wellbeing, not only outside but inside. *Christ is here, it's okay. In the midst of your problems, it's okay. Peace.*

And when Jesus said "shalom"—or "salaam"—He wasn't just saying, "Hi, have a nice day"—*He was bestowing His peace.*

Will you believe that? Will you discipline your heart to take what He offers?

> Thou wilt keep him in perfect peace, whose mind is stayed on thee. (Isa. 26:3 KJV)—or "whose eyes are fixed on You"!
>
> Now may the Lord of peace himself give you peace at all times and in every way. (2 Thess. 3:16)
>
> *Fix Your Eyes on Jesus*

Right now, eliminate from mind even the closest circle surrounding you, and concentrate on your soul. Surrender to God. Relax; sink down into His terms. Let Him create in your spirit beauty and peace and rest.

> Hidden in the hollow of His blessed hand,
> Never foe can follow, Never traitor stand;
> Not a surge of worry, Not a shade of care,
> Not a blast of hurry Touch the spirit there.
>
> Stayed upon Jehovah, Hearts are fully blest;
> Finding, as He promised, Perfect peace and rest.*
>
> *Disciplines of the Heart*

---

*Frances R. Havergal (1836–1879), "Like a River Glorious."

Because of Christ's resurrection He offers you His purpose.
One of the first things He said in His resurrection body was this:

> "As the Father has sent me, I am sending you." (John 20:21)

A brand new principle was suddenly at work!

Back in His earthly life He'd often say, "Now, don't tell anyone about Me" (Mark 1:34, 43; 3:12; 5:43; 7:36; 8:30; and so on). From our side of the resurrection, that seems absolutely strange.

But when Christ exploded out of that grave, all His followers exploded into action. "Go!" He said. "Tell! Be My witnesses to the ends of the earth!" (Matt. 28:19; Acts 1:8).

The resurrection not only changed *Him*, it changed *them*. Boy, did they go! Apparently only one of the Twelve died in his homeland. They went everywhere, "and preached the word wherever they went" (Acts 8:4). Acts is the book of action.

His new purpose was now their new purpose.

His new life was their new life.

They were now in Him, and He was now in them.

Jesus' resurrection—it meant everything! He's risen; He's alive!

Fix your eyes on Him: What's He telling you to do?
GOFORIT.

Fix Your Eyes on Jesus

Because of Christ's resurrection He offers you His power.
Let me give you here a very important truth for your living:

Your weaknesses—totally acknowledged and continually realized—give you your only claim and access to His resurrection power.

I've been a Christian since I was about six years old, and I don't think I'm any stronger now than when I was six. And it's all right with me.

Are you weak? The Lord doesn't take that weakness away. He says, "My power is made perfect in weakness" (2 Cor. 12:9).

And Paul's response to this was, "Therefore I will boast all the more gladly about my weaknesses, so that Christ's power may rest on me. . . . When I am weak, then I am strong" (2 Cor. 12:9–10).

Don't be concerned or embarrassed over your weaknesses. Don't try to forget them or hide them or pray to conquer them or be freed from them.

Jesus doesn't *make you stronger*. The risen Lord said, "You will receive power when the Holy Spirit comes upon you" (Acts 1:8). It's His power only; it always has been, always will be. He doesn't lessen your weaknesses and add a little of His strength, the way I blend a glass of iced tea.

Your total weakness and His total strength are to coexist side by side.

We have this treasure in jars of clay to show that this all-surpassing power is from God and not from us. (2 Cor. 4:7)

Let the only measure of your expectations for yourself be *the resurrection power of Jesus Christ.*

Fix Your Eyes on Jesus

94

*L*et the only measure of your expectations for yourself be the resurrection power of Jesus Christ.

Then you can live a truly powerful life—not because you're no longer weak, but because, being weak, you count on His power to work in you.

We had company for dinner the other night, and the two lamps flanking the couch wouldn't go on. Oh, well . . . But after they'd left, Ray investigated and found the plug in the wall socket was sort of sagging out and had lost its connection.

Never mind your weaknesses; just make sure you're solidly connected, strongly "abiding in Him."

Then *expect the power of His resurrection to work in your life.*

With that he breathed on them and said, "Receive the Holy Spirit." (John 20:22)

Right now, sit loose in your chair.

Breathe out—I'm doing it, too—as if expelling your lack of confidence in His abilities on your behalf.

Now prayerfully breathe in, in a sense, a fresh filling of His Holy Spirit. Breathe in new expectations of His victories in your life.

Prayer:
O wonderful Lord Jesus Christ of the empty tomb,

>I receive anew Your presence.
>
>I receive anew Your peace.
>
>I receive anew Your purpose.
>
>I receive anew Your power.
>
>>In Your own dear name,
>>Amen.

Fix Your Eyes on Jesus

95

*T*hink about your resurrection in Christ.

First let's illustrate it this way. When God created the world, He created it with history already built in. The stars, and also the light from the stars—that light that takes thousands of light-years to get to earth—everything was created in one act. God created it "old."

When He created man, He created him, too, with history already built in. Adam was created a full adult; he didn't go through the process of growing up. He was made in an instant with an age factor already built in.

When you were born again, you were placed into Christ, and the history of Christ was accounted, was credited, to you. You were given the advantages of His history, so that the experiences Christ Himself went through are now yours as well.

That's what Colossians 3 says; now live like it!

> Since, then, you have been raised with Christ, set your hearts on things above, where Christ is seated at the right hand of God. Set your minds on things above, not on earthly things. (Col. 3:1–2)

"Set your *minds* on things above," "set your *hearts* on things above." Bishop Lightfoot comments, "You must not only *seek* heaven, you must also *think* heaven."

Sometimes Ray and I, if a problem comes along, say to each other, "Keep looking down!" It always brings a chuckle. If we were to say "keep looking up," we'd be indicating we're in the pits. But what we're doing is reminding each other of our exalted position in the heavenlies in Christ—and everything immediately looks better.

Confident in Christ

96

God "raised [Christ] from the dead and seated him at his right hand in the heavenly realms," says Ephesians 1:20.

Superiors sit; inferiors stand in their presence. And Christ Jesus earned the right, by His death and resurrection, to sit in heaven. The book of Hebrews, emphasizing Jesus' superiority over priests and kings and angels, talks a lot about His being seated:

> After [Christ] had provided purification for sins, he sat down at the right hand of the Majesty in heaven. (1:3)

> We do have such a high priest, who sat down at the right hand of the throne of the Majesty in heaven. (8:1)

> When [Christ] had offered for all time one sacrifice for sins, he sat down at the right hand of God. (10:12)

> [He] endured the cross, scorning its shame, and sat down at the right hand of the throne of God. (12:2)

And in Christ you, too, have great authority. Seated "with him in the heavenly realms in Christ Jesus," His triumph is your triumph, and His place at the Father's right hand is your place! Says Ephesians 2:6,

> And God raised us up with Christ and seated us with him in the heavenly realms in Christ Jesus.

Or as Hannah said it,

> [God] raises the poor from the dust
>   and lifts the needy from the ash heap;
> He seats them with princes
>   and has them inherit a throne of honor.
>   (1 Sam. 2:8)

Confident in Christ

God raised us up with Christ and seated us with him in the heavenly realms in Christ Jesus. (Eph. 2:6)

*B*eing seated with Christ means that you're in—

A *place of honor*. As the Son, "the radiance of God's glory," sits down at the right hand of that Heavenly Majesty (Heb. 1:3), so you, in God's eyes, are radiant with the glory of Christ and share His prestigious seat (Eph. 2:6).

A *place of rest*. As Christ, the great High Priest, has finished His work and can do no more (Heb. 10:12–13), so *in Him* you will never again have to work—that is, strive to be acceptable to Him. Away with anxiety that your church attendance, your giving, your serving might not be quite enough to earn God's favor! He says in Christ you can rest (Heb. 4:3).

A *place of learning*. As the Son in His earthly life sat daily in the temple teaching (Matt. 26:55), so you, too, have an amazing "anointing" (1 John 2:27), the very "mind of Christ" (1 Cor. 2:16). Of course you need to study; of course a "know-it-all" attitude would be obnoxious. Actually, when we realize all God says He has given us in Christ, we can only be filled with worship and wonder.

A *place of intercession*. As the Son has the intimate ear of Almighty God (Heb. 7:25), so you have that same place of un-believable privilege, so that you can ask what you will and it shall be done (1 John 3:22; 5:14–15).

A *place of fellowship*. As the Lord Jesus in His earthly life loved sitting and talking to Mary (Luke 10:39), so He does now with you!

> And He talks with me,
>   and He tells me I am His own;
> And the joy we share
> As we tarry there
>   None other has every known.

Confident in Christ

*R*ay was walking one day on the beach near our Southern California home, thinking about the power of God in our lives.

Just then he happened to come upon a dead sea gull washed up on the shore. He thought, "If I threw the carcass of this gull up into the air, gravity would make it fall to the ground with a thud. On the other hand, over my head sea gulls are flying everywhere."

What was the difference? It was life. The power of gravity was just as great on the living gulls as on the dead ones, but the greater power of life within lifted the living ones and overcame gravity's downward drag.

So Romans 8:9–11 says,

> You . . . are controlled not by the sinful nature but by the Spirit, if the Spirit of God lives in you. . . . And if the Spirit of him who raised Jesus from the dead is living in you, he who raised Christ from the dead will also give life [that lifting, overcoming life-force] to your mortal bodies.

God's resurrection power is the greatest upward force of all forces; that's the power of godliness that He's put within your very own body.

And the apostle Paul prays that you will *understand this power*, dear person feeling downward pulls in your life! So few do understand—and understanding makes all the difference.

He prays "that the eyes of your heart may be enlightened" (would you ask God to open the eyes of your heart?)—

> that you may know . . . his incomparably great power for us who believe. That power is like the working of his mighty strength, which he exerted in Christ when he raised him from the dead. (Eph. 1:18–20)

Disciplines of the Heart

*L*ast Sunday's sermon (not one of Ray's) included a story about an eagle egg lost from its nest and put into the nest of a prairie chicken. So the egg was hatched with the rest, and the little eagle grew up thinking he was a prairie chicken, too. He scratched in the dirt with the rest for seeds and worms, and he flew in just brief stretches by a great deal of thrashing with his wings.

One day when the eagle was grown, he saw a great eagle soaring in the sky.

"What's that?" he asked in wonder, watching the eagle catch the air currents, almost without effort.

"Oh, that's an eagle," was the answer. "You and I can never be like that."

And so he never was. And he lived his life and died, thinking he was a prairie chicken.

Children Are Wet Cement

Since, then, you have been raised with Christ, set your hearts on things above, where Christ is seated at the right hand of God. Set your minds on things above, not on earthly things. For you died, and your life is now hidden with Christ in God. (Col. 3:1–3)

*T*hrough the pains in your life, through your embarrassment over your sins, through your insecurities, through the times you botch up your relationships with those around you—don't you need a place to hide, a place to get cleansed and forgiven, a place of comfort, a safe spot where you can withdraw and regroup?

The Christian has such a place: Christ Himself.

> "In Christ" denotes your position:
> > where He is, you are.
> "In Christ" defines your privileges:
> > what He is, you are.
> "In Christ" describes your possessions:
> > what He has, you share.
> "In Christ" determines your practice:
> > what He does, you do.

Listen—the heart, the inner kernel, of Christianity isn't knowledge. It isn't church loyalty. It isn't ethics. *The essence of Christianity is the life lived in Christ.*

Move out beyond a mere intellectual knowledge of a historical Christ. Move even beyond accepting His payment of death on the cross for your sin, so that your name is on God's membership list.

Those two little words "in Christ" probably better define you as a Christian than any others, and no other description of you has ever had such lofty meanings or such far-reaching implications.

By an act of your will and by your daily experience, begin to live and move and have your being *in Him.* As Huegel says it, "Dispossessed of your life, become . . . possessed of a Divine life."*

Confident in Christ

---

*F. J. Huegel, *Bone of His Bone.*

One of the tours to Israel the two of us have led included a time in Switzerland. Our overnight in a Swiss hotel was the high point. It was winter in the Alps, and we warmed our tummies with a wonderful supper before a roaring fire. Then to bed . . . with a leisurely breakfast the next morning before swimming in the hotel's luxurious indoor swimming pool. The water was deliciously warm.

But two of the four walls were solid glass, with snow piled outside against the bottom of the frames, and a view of mountain slopes in the distance, and skiers swooping down out of the heights and passing just a few feet from our windows. We watched it all—Alps, snow, skiers—submerged in the warm waters of the pool.

Just as it made all the difference in that Swiss hotel—in what we wore, in our behavior—whether we were "out" in the snow or "in" the pool, so being "in Christ" makes all the difference in your Christian life. All your equilibrium as a Christian, all your true understanding of relationships and destiny and functions, comes from understanding *where you are*. When you *understand where you are*, what it means to be "in Christ," you'll understand how you're to be equipped and what you're to do as a result.

Confident in Christ

He who dwells in the shelter of the Most High
    will rest in the shadow of the Almighty.
I will say of the LORD, "He is my refuge and my
        fortress,
my God, in whom I trust." (Ps. 91:1–2)

*W*hat does being in Christ imply?

It implies incredible closeness to Him. When you're in Christ, you are a part of Him, you are connected with Him. You can't get any closer than that!

Paul knew that in a Roman prison, on a storm-beaten ship, at Caesar's judgment hall—wherever he was, all was well. Why? Because "in him we live and move and have our being" (Acts 17:28). Much later, Tennyson put it this way:

> Speak to Him, thou, for He hears,
>   And Spirit with Spirit can meet.
> Closer is He than breathing,
>   And nearer than hands and feet.

If you're feeling at this moment that God is far away from you, we're not on the subject of "feelings." Never base what you believe on what you experience, but only on what God's Word says is true. Whether you feel it or not, Christian, *God is close to you and you are close to God*—closer than close.

> If that thrills you, it's true.
> If it doesn't thrill you, it's still true.

As you learn to walk by faith and not by sight, a deep sense of peace and well-being will begin to pervade your soul. You'll know, like Paul, that *wherever you are, all is well*—because you are close, close to Him.

You are IN HIM.

Confident in Christ

*B*ecause believers are rooted in Him," says *The Daily Walk*, "built up in Him, dead with Him, risen with Him, alive with Him, hidden in Him, and complete in Him, it is utterly inconsistent for them to live a life without Him. Clothed in His love, with His peace ruling in their hearts, they are equipped to make Christ preeminent in every walk of life."*

Be "in Him" for your relationships. ("Lord, You have put _____ into my life. How can I bless him/her in every contact? How can I grow, and how can I help him/her to grow, as we relate to each other?")

Be "in Him" for your righteousness. ("Lord, help me to accept your chastening to burn away my unpleasant characteristics; and strengthen my traits and my deeds that please You.")

Be "in Him" for comfort. ("Lord, I accept grief in my life as from Your hand. But don't let me grieve as those who have no hope. Praise You that Your name is Comforter!")

Be "in Him" for guidance, deliverance, healing, help. ("Lord, in this situation, in each circumstance of my life today, may my reflex action be instant prayer, instant fleeing to You.")

Abide in Him—for everything good and wonderful for you. Be constantly affirming, "Lord, You are my hiding place."

Confident in Christ

The Daily Walk, 30 November 1986.

*L*ord, how wonderful my hiding place
    In Christ, in Jesus Christ!
Fortified am I from time and space,
Secretly secured by covering grace,
    In Jesus Christ.

Those who seek will find the most, the best
    In Christ, in Jesus Christ;
Joy they'll find, and strength enough, and rest,
Peace within the midst of strain and test
    In Jesus Christ.

        Kingdoms totter, powers crash and fall;
        Mortal schemers face a flaming wall!
        Alpha and Omega, Faithful, True,
        I am hidden safe, secure in You.

All God's treasure-stores are only found
    In Christ, in Jesus Christ;
All the universe's silent sound,
Time, eternity, and truth are bound
    In Jesus Christ.

Soon will sin's rebellions all be stilled
    In Christ, in Jesus Christ;
Soon will hosts of heaven, amazed and thrilled,
See the ancient prophets' words fulfilled
    In Jesus Christ!

        Kingdoms totter, powers crash and fall;
        Mortal schemers face a flaming wall!
        Alpha and Omega, Faithful, True,
        I am hidden safe, secure in You.
                            —*Anne Ortlund*

                    Confident in Christ

*W*e had a bunch of letters to mail the other day, and Ray put them into his Bible so he wouldn't forget to mail them. But his Bible went from his hand into his briefcase, and his briefcase went with him aboard a plane to Fresno, California, where he was to speak. When he got to his hotel and opened his Bible, out fell those letters. They were *in* his Bible—so everything that happened to his Bible happened to the letters.

In the same way, Christian, you are *in* Christ Jesus, and everything that has happened to Him has happened to you.

This makes you more involved in the cross of Christ than you may have first realized. Many Christians' only comprehension of His crucifixion is that the penalty for their sins was death (Gen. 2:17; Rom. 5:12), and that God gave His only Son Jesus to pay that penalty for them (John 3:16).

So far they're right, and those truths are wonderful. But then do we just walk away scot-free, brushing off our hands? Do we just say, "Thanks a lot, Lord"—and that's the end of it? Those two little words *in Christ* open the door to much more than that. When Christ died, you and I died. Whatever happened to Him is counted as happening to us.

> Don't you know that all of us who were baptized into Christ Jesus were baptized into his death? (Rom. 6:3)

Confident in Christ

Near the cross! O Lamb of God,
  Bring its scenes before me;
Help me walk from day to day
  With its shadows o'er me.

—*Fanny J. Crosby*

God has invented the most incredible word to explain the oneness you have with Christ. He uses it in 1 Corinthians 12:13 when He says that all believers have been *baptized* by one Spirit into Christ.

One Greek-English lexicon says *to baptize* means "to immerse, to plunge, to drench, to overwhelm."* Using the word positively, the Holy Spirit has "overwhelmed you" with the love and grace of Christ. He has enveloped you in Christ for the purpose of your complete, eternal transformation; He has overpowered you; He has *baptized* you into Christ.

What is your true identification, you who read this? Is it that you're a woman, a black, a banker, a bricklayer, or the spouse of someone famous? Is it that you have a rare disease? Is it that you once won a great athletic championship or played in Carnegie Hall? Is it that you're in line to be an astronaut or a U.S. president, or that you're soon going into a convalescent home?

No, your identification isn't what you used to be or what you hope to be or even what you now are "in the flesh." Those things mean little, for good or bad, compared with your eternal, incomparable stature and importance and value being in Christ.

Confident in Christ

Like an apple tree among the trees of the forest
    is my lover among the young men.
I delight to sit in his shade,
    and his fruit is sweet to my taste.
He has taken me into the banquet hall,
    and his banner over me is love.
Strengthen me with raisins,
    refresh me with apples, for I am faint with
        love.
His left arm is under my head,
    and his right arm embraces me. (Song of Sol. 2:3–6)

---

*Arndt and Gingrich, ed., *Greek-English Lexicon of the New Testament*.

107

*T*he two of us fell in love on our very first date, a moonlight horseback ride on an August evening. We went home that very night and wrote our parents that we'd found our marriage partners—even though we didn't tell each other.

On December 9 we sealed our desire to marry with Psalm 34:3 (KJV)—"O magnify the LORD with me, and let us exalt his name together"—and became officially engaged with a ring on Christmas morning. We dated every chance we got. We were truly, truly in love.

A year and a half later we married. Our hearts and lives began to lock together in lifelong identification. We shared one name. We became one flesh.

Today our identification is still certainly official, but after all these years it's much more than that. We are completely under each other's influence and power. We are truly subject to each other. We are deeply changed by one another. We are totally identified in each other's character and work. We know intimately each other's bodies, and much of each other's souls. We wouldn't dream of deliberately defying the other's wishes or of hiding major secrets. The implications of our oneness have become too many to count. We are bonded.

But *baptizo* means far more. This Greek term exposes depths of identification that married partners have never thought of. In infinitely more profound ways, *baptizo* describes how the Spirit brings you under the power and character and influence of Christ, not just for a lifetime but for eternity. As believers we are mysteriously bonded to Him, enveloped in Him, "baptized" into His life and work until we're changed totally, unalterably, and forever.

Confident in Christ

We were all baptized by one Spirit into one body, . . . and we were all given the one Spirit to drink. (1 Cor. 12:13)

108

In Christ all the fullness of the Deity lives in bodily
form, and you have been given fullness in Christ, . . . having been buried with him in baptism and raised with him
through your faith in the power of God, who raised him from
the dead. (Col. 2:9–10, 12)

*B*aptizo describes how the Spirit brings you under the
power and character and influence of Christ, not just for a lifetime but for eternity. As believers we are mysteriously bonded
to Him, enveloped in Him, "baptized" into His life, death, resurrection, and work until we're changed totally, unalterably,
and forever.

Your baptism into Christ lifts you, with Him, into God's
eternal scheme of all things.

"In Christ" is not a slogan to catch your attention. It's not
on the level of "Things go better with Coke." It's not an addi-
tive to make your Christian life a little better, like putting extra vitamins in your milk.

In Christ is the very shape of Christianity's scheme of
things.

It's the truth you celebrate.
It's the ground you stand on.
It's the heritage you claim.

You can't rephrase it; you can only live it and enjoy it.

It's the reason you thrill at the thought, *"O Christ, You are
my hiding place!"*

Confident in Christ

109

*O*ur friend Phyllis worked for many years as a missionary in the jungles of Mexico among Indians with almost a stone-age culture. She had no electricity, no running water, no transportation.

One furlough Phyllis helped care for a woman dying of cancer. The woman finally died, after which her widower John fell in love with Phyllis. Eventually the two of them were married.

Phyllis is no longer a missionary in the jungles. John was a globally famous surgeon, and Phyllis now shares everything John is and has. She shares his home, his connection, his wealth, his fame. Now he's retired and she shares his new lifestyle, his travels, his leisure, his interests, and his friends. She bears John's name, and her life mingles with his life. Her identity is his identity.

But Phyllis's new life is not nearly as radical a promotion as yours in Christ.

An embryo shares the body and life and nourishment of its mother. A branch shares everything in common with the vine. No illustration ever says it all, but you now share everything with Jesus Christ.

Your life mingles with His life, and you are given fullness in Him (Col. 2:10)—the same fullness that He shares with the Father (Col. 1:19).

You are powerfully, totally baptized into Christ.

Confident in Christ

*W*hat will your life look like if you abide in Christ?

1. *In times of trouble* you'll relax in Him:

The LORD is a refuge for the oppressed
  a stronghold in times of trouble. (Ps. 9:9)

We acted emotionally a while back. Without taking time
for prayer, we cosigned for a friend's loan, which Proverbs says
never to do. Then the friend went bankrupt, and the lending
institution cleaned out our life savings. For several years we
thought we'd lose even our home.

But it was wonderful what a refuge He was! We nestled in
His arms. He was our stronghold in that time of trouble.

2. *When someone's maliciously going after you*, you'll burrow
deeper into Christ.

O LORD my God, I take refuge in you;
  save and deliver me from all who pursue me. (Ps. 7:1)

In the third of our twenty years pastoring Lake Avenue
Congregational Church, three women decided we were pro-
Communist. They wrote letters to all three thousand members—including all the missionaries who hadn't been home yet
and who worried over their new "liberal" pastor. They delivered
to the door of every member a petition to have us removed; they
brought us before the governing board.

Through that difficult year we never defended ourselves (1
Pet. 2:21–23; Isa. 53:7). Now looking back, we see how God
delivered us. He was our refuge.

Yes, when your reputation is wrongly threatened, your defense will be in Christ.

Confident in Christ

111

Hiding in Thee,
    hiding in Thee,
Thou blest Rock of Ages,
    I'm hiding in Thee.

—William O. Cushing

*W*hat will your life look like if you abide in Christ?
When bad circumstances threaten, you won't get the jitters—you'll pray,

Keep me safe, O God,
    for in you I take refuge. (Ps. 16:1)

When you're plagued with guilty feelings, you'll go back to His promises:

No one will be condemned who takes refuge in him (Ps. 34:22).

This was true for our friend Mark, who wrestles with a thousand insecurities. He was raised in an orphanage, has no knowledge of where he came from or who, humanly speaking, he is. Even in the orphanage he was despised and finally he ran away. Nameless, penniless, colorless, Mark has become renowned, rich, colorful.

Inside, his human tendency is to degrade himself, to worry and wonder and push too hard and think it's never enough. Without Christ Mark could have become suicidal. But he continually gives his inner terrors to Jesus; to pray with Mark is a tremendous experience. His position "in Christ" has flung up a taut, straining, but joyous sail and given him full-speed-ahead power.

Confident in Christ

*W*hat will your life look like if you abide in Christ?
In times of danger you can be absolutely lighthearted:

> But I will sing of your strength,
>   in the morning I will sing of your love;
> for you are my fortress,
>   my refuge in times of trouble. (Ps. 59:16)

In short, *in Christ you can be unflappable:*

> He alone is my rock and my salvation;
>   he is my fortress, I will never be shaken.
> My salvation and my honor depend on God. (Ps. 62: 6–7)

There in Christ, at last, you see where your joy is to come from:

> Let all who take refuge in you be glad;
>   let them ever sing for joy. (Ps. 5:11)

The Old Testament calls Him a refuge, a fortress, a stronghold; the psalms are full of this thought. We count sixty-one times there that those words describe Him—in addition to other psalms that say, "The LORD's unfailing love surrounds the man who trusts in him" (Ps. 32:10); "In the shelter of your presence you hide them" (Ps. 31:20); "You have been our dwelling place" (Ps. 90:1); "He who dwells in the shelter of . . . will rest in the shadow of . . ." (Ps. 91:1); "I hide myself in you" (Ps. 143:9).

The New Testament spells out the specific name of this mighty refuge: It's Jesus! Halleluia!

Confident in Christ

You also were included in Christ when you heard the word
of truth, the gospel of your salvation. Having believed, you
were marked in him with a seal, the promised Holy Spirit.
(Eph. 1:13)

*W*hat would have to happen to you, once you're placed
by the Father into Christ, for you to lose your standing in Him?

*Someone would have to break the seal of God's ownership of
your life.* Ephesians 1:13 gives a succession of steps in the act of
salvation:

a. You heard the word of truth;

b. You believed;

c. You were included in Christ;

d. You were marked in Him with a seal, the Holy Spirit.

For you to lose your standing in Christ, someone would
have to break the hold of the Holy Spirit, a seal stronger than
any seal on earth.

Break the seal of God's Spirit? Impossible!

Place me like a seal over your heart,
    like a seal over your arm;
for love is as strong as death,
    its jealousy unyielding as the grave.
It burns like blazing fire,
    like a mighty flame.
Many waters cannot quench love;
    rivers cannot wash it away.
    (Song of Sol. 8:6–7)

O love that will not let me go,
I rest my weary soul in Thee.

Confident in Christ

114

*T*he Lord Jesus Christ is personally the glue of the Cosmos. He "holds everything together," says Colossians 1:17 (TLB). And Hebrews 1:3 says He "[sustains] all things by his powerful word."

But more. You yourself, believer, are particularly held by Him. Your body, soul, and spirit are held, truly held. Do you know how "held" you are?

"I am always with you," prays the psalmist; *"you hold me"* (Ps. 73:23).

A thousand years later Christ nods, "Yes, I hold in My very hand *all* My children, and—

No one can snatch them out of my hand. My Father, who has given them to me, is greater than all; no one can snatch them out of my Father's hand. (John 10:28–29)

Christ holds you; the Father holds you. The two hands merge into one clasp, and you are utterly secure. Relax in that truth. Mentally, physically, right now rest in it. *You are held.*

I am precious in His sight—
  He will hold me fast;
Those He saves are His delight,
  He will hold me fast!

                              —*Ada R. Habershon*

"But what if I slip out of His fingers?" someone asked. And the answer came, "You *are* one of His fingers!"

Such is God's holding. Wonder of wonders, in Christ you become part of Him!

Confident in Christ

115

Before the hills in order stood,
  or earth received her frame,
From everlasting Thou art God,
  to endless years the same.

O God, our help in ages past,
  our hope for years to come,
Be Thou our guide while life shall last,
  and our eternal home!
                                    —*Isaac Watts, 1719*

A fellow once visited his friend, a music teacher. The visitor said, "Well, what's the good news today?" The teacher went over to a tuning fork, struck it, and said, "That, my friend, is A. It was A all day yesterday. It will be A all day today, tomorrow, next week, and for a thousand years. The soprano upstairs warbles off-key. The tenor next door flats on the high notes. The piano across the hall is often out of tune. But that"—striking the tuning fork again—"that is A. That's the good news today!"

Christian, the truth is that Christ is "A"! When you abide in Him, you are where it's at! Terrible grammar but magnificent truth.

Change and decay in all around I see;
  O Thou Who changest not, abide with me.

Christ abides with you, and you abide with Him, and the position of both of you is immovable.

Confident in Christ

*O*h, *how steady, how consistent, how reliable is your Lord Jesus!* His love is unchanging: Jeremiah 31:3. His Word is unchanging: 1 Peter 1:24–25. His throne is unchanging: Hebrews 1:8. His salvation is unchanging: Hebrews 7:24–25. His gifts to you are unchanging: James 1:17. He Himself is unchanging: Malachi 3:6.

And you want to be like Jesus. Do you sense that your life has a steadiness to it? Or do you want it to? *What is it about your life that's up-and-down?*

Your weight? Join Weight Watchers or some other group to hold you accountable.

Your affection for your marriage partner, roommate, someone else close? Ask a steady, older, godly person to disciple you. Meet with that one regularly, confess your problem, solicit prayer, and report each time how you're doing.

Your emotions? Get a physical checkup, telling your doctor your specific symptoms.

Your Bible reading and prayer life? Join a small group (four to eight people) to whom you can answer. Ask to be checked up on.

Wherever in yourself you sense a tendency to instability, quickly reach to an outside source and deliberately build in accountability consistence.

The point is, *Begin to mold your life to His;* start to reflect Him. "Seek his face always" (Ps. 105:4). Soon you, too, will begin to project His kind of wonderful reliability, flow, steadiness, dependability, continuity.

Then "Continue in the grace of God"! (Acts 13:43). "Continue in his kindness"! (Rom. 11:22). "Continue in your faith"! (Col. 1:23). "Continue to live in him"! (Col. 2:6). Continue in faith, love and holiness"! (1 Tim. 2:15). "Continue in what you have learned"! (2 Tim. 3:14). "Continue in him"! (1 John 2:28).

Fix Your Eyes on Jesus

117

Υou've looked through a toy kaleidoscope, and as you twisted the tube, the bits of colored glass kept repatterning over and over. Look at Jesus Christ to see God's glory, and that glory will be "new every morning," always different, always beautiful.

"Show me your glory," Moses begged the Lord God. "No man can see my face and live," said God. "But I will put you in a cleft in [a certain] rock and . . . you will see my back" (Exod. 33:18–23). (His *back?* Moses had asked to see His *glory*. God is so mysterious.)

When God put Moses there in the rock, what was the glory of God that He allowed Moses to see? That God is "the LORD, the LORD, the compassionate and gracious God, slow to anger, abounding in love and faithfulness, maintaining love to thousands, and forgiving wickedness, rebellion and sin. Yet he does not leave the guilty unpunished" (Exod. 34:6–7).

You're looking through the kaleidoscope at Jesus Christ, "the radiance of God's glory." Twist the tube a little. Oh—He's the LORD, transfigured before Peter, James, and John. His face shines like the sun, and His clothes become as white as the light. . . Twist the tube. Oh—*He is the compassionate God.* Two blind men are before Him, begging, "Lord, we want our sight." And Jesus touches their eyes and they see . . . Twist the tube. Look: *He's not leaving the guilty unpunished.* He's found money-changers in the temple; He's made a whip out of cords, and He's overturning their tables and driving them out! . . . Twist the tube. "*Abounding in love and faithfulness*": Now He's feeding the five thousand hungry people. Twist . . . "*Gracious*": He's taking children into His arms . . . Keep twisting and twisting, and every time you stop, you'll see another radiant facet of the glory of God.

And yet all this, so far, is only His back! *What will be the rest of God's glory, which will be revealed when you see His face?!*

Fix Your Eyes on Jesus

Do you think anything concerning you right now is too small?
   Your house or apartment?
   Your personal reputation? Your influence?
   Your job?
   Your family (you want to add a spouse or children)?
   Your circle of friends?
   Your salary?
   Your *life*?

Until I paid attention to Psalm 131 I chafed. Then I discovered that God's leash wasn't too tight—my heart was too proud! I thought I "deserved" more; my self-image had greater expectations, and that attitude was the very grease on which I slid into self-pity, discontent, ungratefulness, misery.

Then I *fixed my eyes on Jesus*—and in my own eyes I became smaller and smaller. What was my stature, my purity, my power, my excellence compared with His?

I felt foolish, embarrassed, very small.

And now what did I deserve? Nothing—nothing at all. I was an "unworthy servant" (Luke 17:10).

Now I looked at all that the Lord God in His incredible grace had lavished on me—with such love and joy—and it was like Christmas in July!

Fix Your Eyes on Jesus

My heart is not proud, O LORD,
   my eyes are not haughty;
I do not concern myself with great matters
   or things too wonderful for me.
But I have stilled and quieted my soul;
   like a weaned child with its mother,
   like a weaned child is my soul within me. (Ps. 131:1–2)

*N*otice *what God can do for small people.*
When Gideon told the Lord that he was small—

My clan is the weakest in Manasseh, and I am the least in my
family (Judg. 6:15)

—then God could give him a big place: He made him leader of his
people.
When Saul said to God that he was small—

Am I not a Benjamite, from the smallest tribe in Israel, and
is not my clan the least of all the clans of the tribe of Ben-
jamin? (1 Sam. 9:21)

—then God could give him a huge place: He anointed him king
over all Israel.

(Later God reminded him why He could elevate him: Be-
cause "you were . . . small in your own eyes"—1 Sam. 15:17.
When he turned proud, the Lord demoted him again.)
When you're dissatisfied, where are your eyes?

*Discontent drives you to want more and more, to expect more
and more, and to develop a spirit of disappointment both with your
own life and with God—which is death to your soul.*

> Lust in final form spends everything
> To purchase headstones.
> All passions die in graveyards.*

Fix your eyes again on your blessed Jesus. He is full of grace
and goodness; trust Him. *Be satisfied. Be thankful.*

Fix Your Eyes on Jesus

---

*Calvin Miller, A Symphony in Sand.

*W*hat if you truly get a view of God? Holy Toledo! He's not a funny, shuffling little old man in the movies.

He is tenderness and mercy. He is holiness—blinding white. He is the loftiness of power, laughing derisively at rebellious nations and biding His time. He is the hot, sudden violence of wrath. The slow, tumbling aeons of ages are in His scope. He is intimacy and fun with His loved ones. He is the blazing jealousy, the sweet, groaning pain, the tender wonder of lovers' love.

Ezekiel caught a glimpse—and fell face downward.
John did, too—and fell down as though dead.
So did Isaiah—and he cried, "I'm ruined!" (Though in a moment God cleansed him, and then he wanted to serve Him forever.)
Yes, if we come to understand anything about God, our sins become enormous to us! King David cried,

> My guilt has overwhelmed me
>   like a burden too heavy to bear. . . .
> I am bowed down and brought very low;
>   all day long I go about mourning. (Ps. 38:4, 6)

And Ezra! He identified himself so with all the wicked people around him that he fell to his knees and prayed,

> "O my God, I am too ashamed and disgraced to lift up my face to you, my God, because our sins are higher than our heads and our guilt has reached to the heavens." (Ezra 9:6)

Joanna: A Story of Renewal

*A*ll of us spend a lot of time in earthly pursuits. But sometimes does your heart hunger for something more? And do you wonder what you're missing? This little life of yours is just a piece of eternity. What are they doing on the other side? They're worshiping God! They're on their faces before him. Revelation 4 and 5 tell about it. In concentric circles, far out to limitless horizons, everyone is gathered around him! Cecil B. De Mille never thought up a scene so grand.

We're just short-sighted, dull little ants busy around a golfball planet, but the Larger Scene, the eternal one, is full of the adoration of God.

When Jesus told us to pray, *"Thy will be done on earth as it is in heaven"*—that's what's happening in heaven: worship! Then worship is obviously, first and foremost, His will.

But be warned. Worshiping God is radical. It's a change in posture—for life. You may look upright on the outside, but in your mind you'll be flat on your face before Him. You'll be continually awed and overwhelmed by Him.

We could mention a lot of positive results, but nevertheless—

One split-second glimpse of who He really is—and you'll feel smashed, ruined, undone, embarrassed, broken.

Joanna: A Story of Renewal

I saw the Lord seated on a throne, high and exalted. . . .
    "Woe to me!" I cried. "I am ruined!" (Isa. 6:1, 5)

When I saw him, I fell at his feet as though dead.
(Rev. 1:17)

122

$\mathcal{W}$e're trying so hard today to worship both God and ourselves, and it seems as if we're failing pretty badly at both.

I have inside of me a hundred temptations to make it my chief goal to be some super-Christian (even worshiping God better than anyone else!), and all the voices around us all would "egg me on" to do it: "The new alchemical dream is: changing one's personality, remaking, elevating, and polishing one's very self . . . and observing, studying, and doting on it."*

What's back of it all? I don't know, except that the reason Lucifer, a chief angel, was thrown out of heaven long ago was that he wasn't satisfied with his status and said, "I will make myself like the Most High."

When Christians are untaught about the highly exalted position they already have in Christ, they fight for self-esteem. But when they see where and who they truly are, they can afford to be humble! We don't exalt ourselves; we must not exalt ourselves. He's already done it for us!

A. E. Whitman said it so well: that if I try to love myself, God loves me more. That if I try to defend and protect myself, God already defends and protects me totally. That if I exalt myself, God exalts me far more. And that it's ridiculous for both of us to be doing it!!

Oh, what an exalted spot He gives us! As He called John in Revelation 4:1 to "come up here" into heavenly realms, so He has given each of us believers the status of owning a private card which admits us at any time into His very presence. But when we realize where we are and look around—up in that high, shining atmosphere of God, we discover that everybody around us has fallen flat on his face (Rev. 7:11)!

Those who realize how *up* they are are the ones who will fall *down*—in humility and worship and adoration.

Joanna: A Story of Renewal

---

*Quoted in the *Pasadena* [Calif.] *Star News*, 24 July 1978.

Offer your bodies as living sacrifices. . . . Then you will be able to test and approve what God's will is—his good, pleasing and perfect will. (Rom. 12:1–2)

*M*eister Eckhart said, "There are plenty to follow our Lord halfway, but not the other half. They will give up possessions, friends, and honors, but it touches them too closely to disown themselves."

Disown yourself! "Not I, but Christ" is the whole secret of abiding in Him. "He must become greater," said John the Baptist; "I must become less" (John 3:30). This may be painful for a moment, but the result is worth it!

Here's how Frank Laubach described his abiding in Christ:

Worries have faded away like ugly clouds, and my soul rests in the sunshine of perpetual peace. I can lie down anywhere in this universe, bathed around by my own Father's Spirit. The very universe has come to seem so homey! I know only a little more about it than before, but that little is all! It is vibrant with the electric ecstasy of God! I know what it means to be "God-intoxicated."*

Get it straight: You are either centered in Christ, abiding in Him, or you're centered in man. There is no alternative. Either Christ is the center of your universe and you are adjusting everything to Him, or you yourself have become the center, and you're struggling to make everything orbit around you and for you, and you're miserable!

Listen—you were made for God!

Confident in Christ

---

*Frank Laubach, *Letters of a Modern Mystic*.

WHAT SHOULD BE IN YOUR HEART
WHEN YOU COME TO CHURCH

1. *Come cleansed.* It's great to know you're going to be squeaky-clean at least once a week. Remember (if you're old enough) Saturday-night baths? Did you wash your hair and polish your shoes too? Weekly worship should do the same thing for your soul.

When Isaiah had a confrontation with God, he discovered right away how dirty he was (Isa. 6:5). As soon as he admitted it God cleansed him, and it was one of the bonuses of coming to God!

Especially before communion times, 1 Corinthians 11:27–32 says that we're particularly to get cleaned up, so that we won't get sick or die as a result of taking it unworthily!

It's the end of the week, and Sunday is approaching. What about you is dirty? Do you need to apologize to someone? Or apologize to God about something? Or rethink before Him some aspect of your life-style that seems besmudged by the world? Get yourself prepared for the high and holy act of coming into His presence with His gathered people.

2. *Come eagerly.* Psalm 52:9 says, "Your name is good. I will praise you in the presence of your saints."

"Eagerly" can be translated "ten minutes early." Or, with fair accuracy it can be translated, "I've decided we're coming back from the mountains Saturday night." Or, "If the guests don't want to join us, they can sleep in." Or, "I'll probably survive this headache if I just go anyway." Or, "Forget TV; I need to be accountable to the Body." Or, "Only the Lord Himself comes ahead of our marriage, dear, but He does come first, and I'll be with you right after church."

3. *Come praying.*

Up with Worship

125

Friend, believe this: God will never let a problem last too long.

> Therefore we do not lose heart. . . . For our light and momentary troubles are achieving for us an eternal glory that far outweighs them all. So we fix our eyes not on what is seen, but on what is unseen. For what is seen is temporary, but what is unseen is eternal. (2 Cor. 4:16–18)

From the large perspective, *pain has a very short life*. This is an immutable principle of God. Look up Isaiah 54:7 and 8, and you'll see it:

> For a brief moment—trouble;
> In the long future—great mercies.
> For a little while—wrath;
> In the long future—everlasting kindness.

Think of the annual Jewish feasts. The mourning feast (the Day of Atonement) lasted a day; the rejoicing one (the Feast of Tabernacles) lasted a week. That's God's style; that's His heart.

Christian, don't fix your eyes on your pain; *fix your eyes on Jesus*.

Wrote Andrew Murray during a hard time,

> First, He brought me here; it is by His will that I am in this difficult place; . . . in that I will rest.
> Second, He will keep me here in His love, and give me grace in this trial to behave as His child.
> Third, He will make the trial a blessing, teaching me the lessons he intends me to learn, and working in me the grace He means to bestow.
> Fourth, in His good time He can bring me out again . . . how and when He knows.
> So . . . I am here by His appointment, in His keeping, under His training, for His time.

You Don't Have to Quit

*A*while back Ray and I went through a really hard period, a time of frustration and depression, and by our own efforts there seemed no way out. We were in prison! Worshiping and praising God and telling each other "perspective, perspective!" seemed our only comforts.

Suddenly, when we were "sleeping," as it were, an angel struck us and said, "Quick, get up," and led us out through opened prison gates (see Acts 12:5–10). Not of our own doing we were free again, and the experience was behind us.

Christian in trouble, *every pain has a short life—but it needs to have its life*.

God could remove your hurt "right-this-minute-no-problem."

In an instant you're healed. (Perhaps He wants to do that.)

Or the one who's starting to bug you quickly moves out of town.

Or you hardly had time to feel a money pinch and you get a glorious raise.

God is powerful enough to do these "miracles." But did you profit enough from the trouble? Did it refine you? Did it teach you the disciplines of patience, perspective, and trust?

A greater miracle might be your holiness.

Consider it pure joy, my brothers, whenever you face trials of many kinds, because you know that the testing of your faith develops perseverance. Perseverance must finish its work so that you may be mature and complete, not lacking anything. (James 1:2–4)

You Don't Have to Quit

The Lord Jesus knew that suffering is part of God's perfect and loving will.

> This suffering is all part of the work God has given you. Christ, who suffered for you, is your example. (1 Pet. 2:21 TLB)

Christians who don't believe their suffering is "of the Lord" turn out weak and unstable. At any encounters with pain they're apt to cry for immediate deliverance, thinking it's of the devil, or else they turn and run—from a job, a church, a marriage, whatever the cause of the pain.

Maybe they've never noticed Philippians 1:29:

> For to you has been given the privilege not only of trusting him but also of suffering for him. (TLB)

Trusting and suffering: The two come as a package. You take one, you get the other with it.

You take salvation from a good Father, you get suffering from the same good Father.

You say "thank you" for one, you say "thank you" for the other (1 Thess. 5:18).

Understanding this simple truth makes strong, sturdy, unflappable believers. Through the worst circumstances their heads are up. Said Job, "Shall we accept good from God, and not trouble?"

Fix Your Eyes on Jesus

> Dear friends, do not be surprised at the painful trial you are suffering, as though something strange were happening to you. But rejoice that you participate in the sufferings of Christ, so that you may be overjoyed when his glory is revealed. (1 Pet. 4:12–13)

God works through pain to bring glory! All of us have to understand that. God's fabulous treasures aren't bought with cash and credit, slapping down a contract on a bargaining table and scratching a signature and a date. They just don't come that way!

Our Lord Jesus suffered, too, to show us the way. He suffered first and most—to purchase for Himself glory in our eyes (Phil. 2:5–11). First the pain, then the prize.

"Come, let us return to the LORD," says the prophet Hosea:

> He has torn us to pieces,
>   but he will heal us;
> he has injured us,
>   but he will bind up our wounds.
> After two days he will revive us;
>   on the third day he will restore us,
>   that we may live in his presence. (6:1–2)

Do you catch something here? It's as if the shadow of a cross is falling across these words. God is totally involved in our suffering, as we will be totally involved in His ultimate triumph. The two processes are inseparable.

Joanna: A Story of Renewal.

We share in his sufferings in order that we may also share in his glory. (Rom. 8:17)

*H*ebrews 12:2 says to "fix your eyes on Jesus" because:

1. "For the joy set before him [he] endured the cross."
And if you, too, "hang in there," your personal glory will follow as well. It won't be long! Jesus "endured." You do the same.

2. But he scorned its shame. Think about this carefully.

To "scorn" means to "belittle." The *cross* Jesus didn't scorn—to suffer on the cross for the sins of the world was Big Deal. And for you to be called by God to participate in His sufferings (1 Pet. 4:13)—that's Big Deal, too. Appreciate it.

But the *shame* of the cross He scorned; He took that part of it lightly. He thought little of His own humiliation, His own feelings. He wasn't self-centered, self-pitying.

If you feel totally misunderstood—or if you have in the past,
If you suffer at the hands of others—or if in the past you did,
Right now, as you're reading this, *pray this prayer:*

"Lord, for my own maturing, to make me more like Christ, You've allowed me to participate in His sufferings. I'm awed. I'm honored to be in such company. That's Big Deal.

"But, Lord, I choose to belittle my own feelings. They're not big deal. Keep me from retaliation, real or imagined; keep me from filling my thoughts with self-pity and fresh self-woundings and all over-occupation with myself.

"Lord, keep my heart and life concerned for others. Lord, give me true compassion for my oppressors. And, Lord, I entrust myself totally to You. Into Your good hands I commit my spirit. Amen."

You're released! You're free! Your heart has begun a *deep process of healing.* Hold your head high!

Fix Your Eyes on Jesus

*W*hat kind of home do you have?

Probably you've got some kind of combination of bodies under your roof: You're a married couple with no kids, a married couple with kids, a single mom or dad with kids; maybe some parents are with you or foster kids or grandchildren—you know your own setup. Ogden Nash says a family unit is composed not only of children but of men, women, an occasional animal, and the common cold.

The big questions aren't, How sharp are all of you? and How much money are you making?

The big questions—no matter how odd your assortment or what their histories or deformities or problems—the big questions are . . .

How do you get along?

How do you help each other and lift each other?

Is your home a place where your young ones can get prepared for tomorrow's world?

Your old ones get comforted?

Your unwise ones get tender guidance?

Your producers get recharged?

Your hurt ones healed?

Or if God has included under your roof any of His lambs who are truly inadequate for this world—is home still where they're loved, where they know they belong?

In other words, is your home a restoring, nourishing, comforting, inspiring place?

God's is, and He wants yours to be.

Disciplines of the Home

. . . And the whole family was filled with joy. (Acts 16:34)

*H*ave you any idea how much God loves families, His own invention? How much He loves your family? How much He loves your kids, who are His, and how concerned He is for them?

In the very beginning of human history God established the family. In fact, three times when He's wanted to begin something special, He's started with a new family:

1. Adam and Eve and their children;

2. After the flood, Noah and his wife and children;

3. After the Tower of Babel, Abraham and Sarah and their offspring.

This third family grew to become the world's most stable social system—a system with father, family, clan, tribe, and nation.

Up the ladder, everyone was *accountable to*.

Down the ladder, everyone was *responsible for*.

Eventually, sin began to split the structure apart, from the top down. Around 600 B.C. the Hebrew nation was broken up and scattered, and with it, its tribes.

Clans went on for centuries, both Jewish and Gentile— extended families living near each other. Eventually, with increased mobility, these, too, were broken up and scattered.

Just since World War II, an escalation in the divorce rate has been breaking up and scattering the next rung down the ladder, the family.

And the status of the father is seriously eroding.

Today's world society is an impending avalanche sliding toward hell. Is your family caught in the slide? Or will you gather your loved ones and make a drastic leap to solid ground?

Disciplines of the Home

Too many humans are wandering around these days having lost a strong sense of what all God's animals understand very well: the difference between male and female.

What happens when we humans start to blur the lines? Society goes bonkers. It's crucial today, in all the body of Christ, for fathers to "act father," mothers to "act mother," the boys to know they're future men, and the girls to know they're future women.

And *three cheers for mother!* Over the centuries she's worked as hard as father, and for very different reasons.

He has built the houses; she's added the colors, the smells, the music.

He has shaped constitutions to make citizens protected; she has sewn flags to make them weep and cheer.

He has mustered armies and police forces to put down oppression; she has prayed for them and patted them on the back and sent them off with their heads up.

He has shaped decisions; she has added morale.

The first man kept a garden, and the first woman was made to be a help "meet"—suitable—for him (Gen. 2:18 KJV). (Does the word "help" sound demeaning? Our God Himself is often called the same word—our help—as in Psalm 33:20.)

The woman in Proverbs 31 got up while it was still dark. She kept everybody fed and clothed. She bought fields. She planted vineyards. She brought in income. She cared for the poor. She was wise. She was busy. She was fun. She was a help, and everybody loved her for it. What did her husband do? He sat at the city gates. Don't laugh! That was the heavy-duty place, the hot spot, the place of governmental and legal and administrative affairs.

Celebrate the mother! She, too, no less than the father, has, under God, shaped a magnificent human tradition.

Disciplines of the Home

$\mathcal{R}$oughly a quarter of all United States households are people living alone, and some other countries report an even higher count. Are you one of these? Whatever your discouragement, whatever your loneliness, your life can become ever richer and sweeter if—

You tackle your problems; you discover that the single life is good, that there are many advantages, and that you're thankful for God's choice for you—at least for the present.

You become more aggressive in nourishing friendships in your life. You get into a small group for accountability and for spiritual and emotional feeding (connectedness was never more important). You discover things you like to do, to replace your previously fuller date life. You help improve the quality of your singles' Sunday school class, or else you get into another adult class where you find that there are more and more singles among the couples, anyway.

If you're widowed or divorced, you consciously end the excessive backward looking and the grieving, and you determine to set new goals and concentrate on the future.

And in all, you learn to trust God that His way for you is best, and you practice the discipline of continual thankfulness.

And if you're not living alone, make sure you encompass into your life, with special thoughtfulness and concern, those who are!

You Don't Have to Quit

I'm looking at a piece of paper here in front of me: a list of thirteen ways the New Testament tells us to communicate with each other. When you eliminate the repetitions, did you know they boil down to only thirteen? Here they are:

1. Suffering together: 1 Corinthians 12:26.
2. Rejoicing together: Romans 12:15.
3. Carrying each other's burdens: Galatians 6:2.
4. Restoring each other: Galatians 6:1.
5. Praying for one another: Romans 15:30.
6. Teaching and admonishing each other: Colossians 3:16.
7. Refreshing one another: Romans 15:32.
8. Encouraging each other: Romans 1:12.
9. Forgiving one another: Ephesians 4:32.
10. Confessing to one another: James 5:15.
11. Being truthful with one another: Ephesians 4:25.
12. Spurring one another toward good deeds: Hebrews 10:24.
13. Giving to one another: Philippians 4:14–15.

And here's the important question for you, under your particular roof: Have you placed yourself so deeply within your family, or those with whom you live, that you're functioning in all these ways, and so living as a well-rounded, healthy, contributing member?

Discipling One Another

*B*ack in Genesis 13:16, when Abraham had settled in the land God had chosen for him, God said to him, "Abram, I will make your descendants as the dust of the earth." In accordance with His "earthly" covenant, God gave him a fabulous promise about his future family: They'd be as plentiful as "earthly" dust.

In Genesis 15:6 Abraham "believed the LORD, and he credited it to him as righteousness," a foundation verse on which all the remainder of "faith teaching" in the Bible rests. And in connection with it, God said, "Abram, your descendants will be as plentiful as the stars."

God repeated His double promise in Genesis 22:17: "I will surely bless you and make your descendants as numerous as the stars in the sky and as the sand on the seashore."

Let's "spiritualize" for a moment God's beautiful analogy of dust and stars. Romans 4:11–18—as well as other places in the New Testament—spells out how God's double promise resulted in a double line of descendants: the Jews, Abraham's earthly descendants by physical heritage, as numerous as dust; and believers, Abraham's heavenly descendants by spiritual heritage, as numerous as stars. Abraham has two great families!

Discipling One Another

> Therefore, the promise comes by faith, so that it may be by grace and may be guaranteed to all Abraham's offspring— not only to those who are of the law but also to those who are of the faith of Abraham. He is the father of us all. . . .
>
> The words "it was credited to him" [Gen. 15:6] were written not for him alone, but also for us, to whom God will credit righteousness—for us who believe in him who raise Jesus our Lord from the dead. (Rom. 4:16, 23–24)

And will you believe God's fresh promises to you personally, this very day?

*T*he whole Old Testament is a story of the development of Abraham's physical descendants, the Jews. Their family structure was strictly physical. They were born into their immediate family, and into a certain clan with a common paternal ancestor, and the clan within one of the tribes, all descended from twelve brothers, and the tribes within the nation Israel, all physically related. In that setup the physical father was also the spiritual head of the home. He was answerable for the sins and successes of the mother and the children; he provided the information for census-taking; he was responsible to teach them and lead them in all things, including spiritual things.

The New Testament, or Covenant, is really new! It brings in a new order. And "by calling this covenant 'new,' he has made the first one obsolete" (Heb. 8:13a). It's the story of Abraham's *spiritual* descendants—those who have believed in God's Son Jesus Christ—and God counts it to them as righteousness, as he did their spiritual father Abraham (Gen. 15:6). There are no physical fathers, clans, or tribes here. No one is born into it by natural birth; we must be "born again" into it, because it's a spiritual family.

Discipling One Another

Everyone who believes that Jesus is the Christ is born of God, and everyone who loves the father loves his child as well. This is how we know we love the children of God: by loving God and carrying out his commands. (1 John 5:1–2)

Oh, we who live under the New Covenant of grace—how blessed we are! "How great is the love the Father has lavished on us, that we should be called children of God!" (1 John 3:1).

*W*hy does Jesus seem so often to rebuff His own physical family (Luke 2:48–50; John 2:4; Luke 11:27–28; Matt. 12:47–50)?

Because He loved His physical family so deeply that He knew a lifestyle of total obedience to God was the only way ultimately to win them! They didn't need His time for time's sake—staying home just to prove Himself a good "brother and son" of the family. They needed to see a life lived wholly for God, and that would be the power they finally couldn't resist.

They did resist for a long time. Mark 3:21 and John 7:5 tell us that during His three years of ministry, they didn't believe in Him. That must have given Him great pangs of loneliness and sadness. But eventually, His unswerving, visible godliness won their hearts!

Look who was in the Upper Room following His ascension, praying and waiting for Pentecost: "They all joined together constantly in prayer, along with the women and Mary the mother of Jesus, and his brothers" (Acts 1:14). Three cheers! When the time finally came to be counted, there they were! And look who became traveling preachers, going everywhere with the new gospel of Jesus Christ! Paul wrote, "Don't we have the right to take a believing wife along with us [when we travel and preach], as do the . . . Lord's brothers?" (1 Cor. 9:5). The power of the life of a physical Brother, Jesus, who gave Himself to God as His highest priority and then to his spiritual family in all of those meaningful and eternally important interactions— that power was finally irresistible, and the physical brothers, too, reached for what they saw in Him.

And look who wrote two Spirit-directed letters which became part of the Word of God: two of the brothers, James and Jude (Matt. 13:55). It must have been a final, wonderful triumph for Jesus to see His own precious physical family become greatly used by God.

Discipling One Another

*T*hink about Jesus' mother, too. She'd been told thirty years before by the prophet Simon that "a sword will pierce your own soul" (Luke 2:35). When her Son was dying on the cross, you'd think that would have been the sword piercing her, but Jesus' words must even have given the sword a twist. He said, "Dear woman, here is your son!" and to John standing by, "Here is your mother!" (John 19:26–27). He Himself was actually making the final break in the physical relationship between them.

Why was Jesus turning his mother over to a new son? Dr. Russell Bradley Jones says,

> The word that grieved Mary so when it was spoken proved, by time's interpretation, to be a blessed word indeed. Mary discovered that she had been led from a natural union *with Jesus* to a mystical union *with Christ*. She gladly took her place among his sincere worshippers. It was not a special place, it was not on a platform; it was with the 120, as a simple believer!
>
> She found that the salvation relationship is higher than the family relationship. She learned that it was better to have Him as her Saviour and Lord than to have Him as her son.
>
> And in a very true sense, she discovered that her former son had made better provision for her as her Saviour than He could have made as her son. Heavenly mansions and eternal life are hardly to be compared with a few fleeting years in John's [home]!*

> *Discipling One Another*

At that first Christmas Mary delivered Jesus. But eventually—halleluia!—Jesus delivered her.

---

*Russell Bradley Jones, *Gold from Golgotha*.

*W*hat does it mean to put God first? It means powerful, revolutionary concepts of living that smash our little pet ideas.

Take Peter, for example. We know he had a home and a wife and a mother-in-law (Luke 4:38)—but there came that last year and a half when the Twelve went "on the road" with Jesus, and that must have seemed tough and maybe even unreasonable. We might tend to think today with our twisted priorities that it just wouldn't be spiritual for Jesus to call a man to leave his family to serve Him—even for roughly eighteen months.

Peter, feeling this deeply at one point, commented, "'We have left all we had to follow you.' 'I tell you the truth?' Jesus said to them, 'no one who has left home or wife or brothers or parents or children for the sake of the kingdom of God will fail to receive many times as much in this age and, in the age to come, eternal life'" (Luke 18:28–30).

The promise here is the exchange of physical family for spiritual family; of a few, for multitudes; of a temporary family for an eternal one; of a family that may inherit a few dollars in the bank for co-heirs with Jesus Christ of all God's glory. Maybe at the moment that didn't seem like much of an exchange to Peter. But he was willing to be obedient, and after a few months' separation, God gave him back a wife who was a new sister in Christ and who was constantly at his side in his preaching and traveling! (1 Cor. 9:5)

What would Peter have missed if he'd put his wife first and refused? Remember the fellow in Jesus' parable who rejected the invitation to dinner because he said, "I just got married, so I can't come"? Jesus said, "I tell you, not one of those men who were invited will get a taste of my banquet" (Luke 14: 20, 24). We shudder to think of all Peter would have lost—and Peter's precious wife, too.

Discipling One Another

140

There is a high road to supplication which staggers the mind. God fills His Word with blank checks:

> Ask and you will receive, and your joy will be complete. (John 16:24)

> This is the assurance that we have in approaching God: that if we ask anything according to his will, he hears us. And if we know that he hears us—whatever we ask—we know that we have what we asked of him. (1 John 5:14–15)

And James 4:2 says that we don't have because we haven't asked.

When George Mueller died, he left a notebook that contained fifty thousand specifically answered prayer requests in it. No wonder God used him!

The words *supplication* and *supply* are connected, and if any believer's life seems poorly supplied in any area at all, it could be because he hasn't really asked God.

There was a time in our first pastorate when we couldn't pay our coal bill. (We had a coal furnace in those days.) We felt bad about it—especially because we owed it to a member of the congregation and had to face him every Sunday! "Dear Lord," Ray and I prayed, "You really have to drop several hundred dollars down out of the blue, because we have no place to get this coal money."

So the Lord had the State of Iowa send us a letter. The State of Iowa has never written us before or since. But God gave Iowa a surplus in its budget right then, and He moved the lawmakers to decide to divide it among Iowa's veterans. And here came a letter of explanation and a check to Ray for the exact amount of the coal bill.

God loves for us to ask.

Joanna: A Story of Renewal

The last section of my notebook, "prayers," is the best of all. How could it have taken me forty-two years of living the Christian life before I ever started writing my prayers? I had absolutely no idea what it was going to do for me.

Before, if you'd asked me what I'd prayed about three days earlier, or maybe an hour earlier, unless it was something crucial, I'd have no idea.

When I started writing prayers I just let the words flow on paper the way they had done out of my mouth, putting down both the important and the seemingly inconsequential. After a few months when I started looking back over what I'd first prayed, I was staggered to discover how seriously God had taken my prayers! A sentence or two, just sort of thrown in, had sometimes started the wheels of heaven turning until the requests had ever-enlarging ramifications and affected ever-enlarging numbers of people! I was learning such a lesson of the power of prayer, it utterly shook me.

A letter from a woman confirmed another feeling of mine about writing down prayers. She said, "Recently when I wrote down for the first time on paper 'I love You, Father,' it had never been more meaningful. It's a completely different feeling from list-making."

Disciplines of the Beautiful Woman

You are kind and forgiving, O Lord,
    abounding in love to all who call to you.
Hear my prayer, O Lord;
    listen to my cry for mercy.
In the day of trouble I will call to you,
    for you will answer me.

*—Psalm 86:5–7, "A prayer of
David," one of many of
David's written prayers,
preserved for God and for us.*

> During the days of Jesus' life on earth, he offered up prayers and petitions with loud cries and tears to the one who could save him from death, and he was heard because of his reverent submission. Although he was a son, he learned obedience from what he suffered. (Heb. 5:7–8)

Study this passage! It's not a lack of confidence in God that makes Christians pray for something and add, "if it's Your will." (Sometimes that's disdained as showing a lack of faith, a way out.) Beware of "claiming" things from God, as if you knew better than He! God's Son was heard "because of his reverent submission." He made a strong request, but He added those words, "If it's Your will, Father" (Matt. 26:39).

And "He was heard," but the Father in infinite wisdom said no.

And listen to what Christ said in Psalm 22, a Messianic Psalm prophesying His death a thousand years in advance: "My God, my God, why have you forsaken me . . . ? O my God, I cry out by day, but *you do not answer*"!

A young pastor friend has in this last year been through the trial of his life. When I saw him recently, he asked me, "What do you do when God doesn't say yes—doesn't give it, doesn't make it happen?"

Then he answered his own question: "Through agony I've gotten to know God better; I love Him more. . . ."

He showed me a piece of paper he keeps in his wallet. It says, "Look to His face, not to His hand."

Joanna: A Story of Renewal

143

𝒩ot only you as a person, but even your prayers must have staying power.

Jesus told about a woman who over and over brought her case before a judge, and he couldn't have cared less about her, but because *she bugged him,* he granted her request.

Jesus' reply was if an uncaring judge will say yes, how much more will your Father, who loves you very much, say yes to you *who cry to him day and night* (Luke 18:7)?

Another time—in fact, when the disciples said, "Lord, teach us to pray" (Luke 11:1)—Jesus taught them what to pray and how.

The "what" was the Lord's Prayer.

The "how"? With persistence. He told another story about another someone who didn't care: This time somebody sleeping in bed who's asked by a friend at midnight (what lousy timing!) for some emergency food. The fellow says, "Don't bother me" (Luke 11:5).

But the friend *bothers him anyway.* And Jesus says the fellow will say yes, *not* because of their relationship—not because they're friends—but only because the guy keeps bugging him!

His conclusion: "If that uncaring friend in bed will say yes, how much more will your Father who loves you very much?"

> "So I say to you: Ask and it will be given to you; seek and you will find; knock and the door will be opened to you." (Luke 11:9)

In other words, "Come on, children, bug Me! Try it! Bug Me!"

You Don't Have to Quit

*D*o you tend to say, "I'm so busy, I really don't have much time for prayer?"

Listen, the issue of prayer really isn't prayer—it's God.

When Ray and I are in a crowded room, we may be doing different things and talking to different people, but we're more or less aware of each other. If one of us has an obvious need, it won't be long until the other has noticed and done something about it. And when other conversations end and other duties get finished, somehow, somehow, we find our way back to each other.

It isn't that we're trying so hard to stay in touch; eventually we'd be exhausted from the intensity of the effort. It's just that we're in love.

The command to "pray without ceasing" may seem like an impossible chore if you're "too busy" for even ten minutes a day. Hear it again: The issue of prayer isn't prayer—it's God. Prayer is simply the measuring device for the state of your relationship with Him.

My friend, fall in love with God.

Disciplines of the Heart

I will sing of your strength,
     in the morning I will sing of your love;
for you are my fortress,
     my refuge in times of trouble.
O my strength, I will sing to you;
     you, O God, are my fortress,
     my loving God. (Ps. 59:16, 17)

I was listening recently to the "Haven of Rest" broadcast. My favorite keyboardist, Duane Condon, was accompanying magnificently, and one of my favorite singers, bass Glenn Shoemaker, was singing "Guide Me, O Thou Great Jehovah."

Duane and Glenn came to verse three, and their music became slower, more majestic, and charged with triumph:

> When I tread the verge of Jordan,
> Bid my anxious fears subside;
> Death of Death and hell's Destruction
> [What magnificent names for Christ!]
> Land me safe on Canaan's side;
> Songs of praises, songs of praises I will ever give
> to Thee!

I thought of my precious friend Becky, in my small group of disciples last year, who just the day before had died of cancer, barely thirty years old. I leaned into the mirror to put cover-up on some wrinkles. And though I love her and I miss her already, I thought, *"You lucky rascal, Becky! You beat me there."*

Of course the pain of losing loved ones is real enough. We don't "grieve like the rest of men" (1 Thess. 4:13), *but we do grieve*— sometimes terribly, deeply, excruciatingly in our loss.

But as far as death goes, we can be absolutely light-hearted. We've been freed from all fear of it (Heb. 2:15); it has no more victory over us, no sting (1 Cor. 15:55).

The Twenty-third Psalm says, "Even though I walk through the valley of the shadow of death, I will fear no evil."

If a truck runs over you, you can get really ruined.

If the *shadow* of a truck runs over you, what happens?

Psalm 23 speaks only of your walking through the *shadow* of death . . . *Is that all?*

In your thinking about dying, get Jesus' perspective.

Fix Your Eyes on Jesus

146

*T*hink of yourself, my friend, as a child of eternity. If the little ones around you are tomorrow's world, in a vaster, far more exciting sense you are eternity's world. *You are part of the future population on the other side.*

Are you getting shaped and trained for it? The Bible is full of descriptions of rewards for those who got ready. Yes, and apparently there is a hierarchy there; Jesus talked a lot about being "greatest in the kingdom" and "least in the kingdom."

Oh, what a solemn thought! I sit here writing to you and praying, "Spirit of the living God, fall afresh on me! Mold me, make me, fill me, use me. . . ."

Surrender yourself totally to God's good work upon you. If you're humble and willing, His power will "unharden" your hardening! He can reverse the process. He can stir the hardening cement and reshape before it finally sets. He can start with you afresh. God is the God of new beginnings.

As long as you're alive, you can soften and begin again under His hands. But when eternity comes—suddenly, in an instant—you will be permanently hardened cement. The Bible ends with these words about the Final Day:

> Let him who does wrong continue to do wrong; let him who is vile continue to be vile; let who does right continue to do right; and let him who is holy continue to be holy. (Rev. 22:11)

At that point everyone will at last be permanently fixed. You've seen it pictured on television: People are moving and talking—and suddenly the scene is frozen into a still shot . . .

And only God knows when His "instant" will be.

Children Are Wet Cement

Our pioneer American forefathers slogged across valleys and mountains and open prairies until they came to a settling place, where they'd stake a claim. Then on the spot they usually put up some rude lean-to until they could build a snug little home out of sod or timber.

What if the wife had said, "Henry, I don't want to move! I don't care if you have built a better place; I just want to keep crawling into this little lean-to for the rest of my life"? Henry would rightly call her crazy.

So God describes our bodies as disposable tents, and he says that fortunately "we have a building from God, an eternal house in heaven, not built with human hands. Meanwhile we groan, longing to be clothed with our heavenly dwelling" (2 Cor. 5:1–2). My word, yes! Who wants girdles and permanents and aches and pains forever?

My friend, detach your affections more and more from what you taste-touch-see. Don't detach your affections from the world itself—you're too needed (Phil. 1:21–26)—but detach yourself from a debilitating closeness to it.

Heaven will be marvelous! Keep it in your mind!

Disciplines of the Heart

Now there is in store for me the crown of righteousness, which the Lord, the righteous Judge, will award to me on that day—and not only to me, but also to all who have longed for his appearing. (2 Tim. 4:8)

I'm very curious about my own death, and very excited over it, and in a great sense eager for it; aren't you?

Dr. Carl Henry has written, "Death is a transition from life to life—that is, from creation life to resurrection life."*And of the two, which is better? Do you go up or down? We have a friend who chuckled, "If Christians had any idea how wonderful heaven is, we'd all commit suicide!"

"What a friend we have"—not only "in Jesus," but in death! Death is your dear friend who will bring you through the door and into the very arms of God.

Then you can keep a light touch on your scheduling ("if it is the Lord's will"—James 4:13–15) and have a holy carelessness about death's interrupting it all.

One time, as a total surprise to Ray, he and I got whisked off by friends for a week in Hawaii. He thought those seven days were solidly filled with appointments and work. But I had secretly rescheduled everything and packed our bags, and before Ray could catch his breath we were suddenly transported to soft Hawaiian sunshine, strains of ukulele music, wonderful food, rest, and fun! Hey, heaven's going to be even better than that!

Death is your transportation into the very arms of God.

Disciplines of the Heart

Creation itself will be liberated from its bondage to decay and brought into the glorious freedom of the children of God. (Rom. 8:21)

---

*"The Road to Eternity," *Christianity Today,* 17 July 1981.

Learn how to live in constant readiness for death.

This means, first of all, not concentrating mostly on your notebook or your wardrobe, but on the disciplines of your heart. That's the inner you—the part that's eternal, and you need to get yourself ready for your entire future.

> My flesh . . . may fail,
>> but God is the strength of my
>>> heart . . . forever. (Ps. 73:26)

You say you're only twenty-three and you can't relate to this? My brother Bobby barely had twenty-four years.

> Man's days are determined;
>> [God has] decreed the number of his months
>> and [has] set limits he cannot exceed. (Job 14:5)

How can you prepare yourself for your own personal death, the only one you'll ever have? By learning to experience solitude. By learning to enjoy being alone. It will get you ready for the ultimate "alone" experience of dying.

If you've clogged and saturated and stuffed your life with unceasing companionship, abundant advice—always the group, always the crowd—you won't know what it is to be an individual. And then if you're suddenly forced to walk single file when it's not familiar, it could be a panicky experience.

Get used to withdrawing. Get used to the sweet presence of Immanuel, who will never leave you nor forsake you.

Solitude is essential if your roots are to grow deep. "Each heart knows its own bitterness, and no one else can share its joy" (Prov. 14:10). "Know thyself"—which means, fortunately, not being an eccentric loner but getting very familiar with being a twosome with God.

Disciplines of the Heart

God does not see the Christian life as role-playing. His Word says that the believer's life is not an imitation of Christ; it's an actual participation in what He has done, is doing, and will do.

Take this in, absorb it, live by it: You participate in His life, and He participates in yours. Your life as a Christian is one with Christ's life. In God's eyes you are totally merged with, identified with, Christ.

Your life really is not separate from His. When He saved you, He didn't reach down from heaven and touch you with a magic wand while remaining remote and aloof. He didn't model righteousness for you, so you could try to imitate Him and "do what Jesus would do" while He stayed in front of you, just out of reach. He didn't save you so He could be merely some kind of Chairman of the Board of your life, or Copilot, or Skipper of your ship, or even your Best Friend. If He had, you could indeed pray, "Lord, be with us."

He is with you, always, forever.

He is within you, living His life; and you are within Him, living your life. In saving you He used an approach none of us could ever have thought up: He became one with you, inseparable from you, fusing His life with yours and yours with His, He in you and you in Him.

Listen: *The essence of Christianity is the life lived in Christ.*

You are always you—and yet you're simultaneously in Christ. Christ is always Christ—and yet He's simultaneously in you.

Christ insists on this kind of love with you, this kind of breathtaking closeness.

Confident in Christ

Υour life in Christ lifts you into a place vastly larger than seen at first glance.

You see, it didn't just begin when you were born again. You were chosen in Him, says Ephesians 1:4, before the creation of the world. You may well ask, "How could I be in Christ—how could God choose me and love me—before He ever made me?"

God isn't caught in time, as we are. He is over all, outside of time, seeing the end from the beginning. So He can pronounce in Revelation 13:8 that Christ is "the Lamb that was slain from the creation of the world." Events are events—and God doesn't think "when" and ask "which came first," the way we do. To Him an act is an act, and it's just as "done" before it appears on the time-line of history as afterward.

So if you're a believer, to God you've always been in Christ.

Seeing your position there, you'll begin to understand how deep, how thorough, how far-reaching, and how important your salvation is to God and to you. This was no willy-nilly decision you made one day, and God, seeing you turn to Him, decided on the spot to forgive your sins and accept you into His family. This was no spur-of-the-moment experience (though it may have seemed so to you) that made God look down and decide to give you one more chance.

Your baptism into Christ lifts you, with Him, into God's eternal scheme of all things.

> So near, so very near to God,
>   Nearer I could not be,
> For in the Person of His Son
>   I am as near as He.
> So dear, so very dear to God,
>   Dearer I could not be;
> The love wherewith He loves His Son
>   Is the love He has for me.

Confident in Christ

152

*H*ow do you abide in Christ? Certainly in your mind, as an act of your will, you decide to abide in Him before you ever understand what you decided. You simply determine to plant yourself "in Christ," to camp day by day on that settled, permanent dwelling spot in which you're going to flourish—sort of like the tree in Psalm 1.

You want to live in vital union with Him because in Him are the perfect conditions for living, like a tree that would never do as well in any other spot. So you let your roots grow down into Him and draw up nourishment from Him.

Colossians 2:9–10 (TLB) tells you why He is the best of all possible soils: "In Christ there is all of God . . . so you have everything when you have Christ, and you are filled with God through your union with Christ." The tree planted deep in Him feeds on all of God.

> The pursuit of God . . . must not be casual. [It's] not a part-time, weekend exercise. . . . Abiding requires a kind of staying power. . . . We sign up for the duration. We do not graduate until heaven.*
>
> *Confident in Christ*

> Blessed is the man who trusts in the LORD,
>   whose confidence is in him.
> He will be like a tree planted by the water
>   that sends out its roots by the stream.
> It does not fear when heat comes;
>   its leaves are always green.
> It has no worries in a year of drought
>   and never fails to bear fruit. (Jer. 17:7–8)

---

*R. C. Sproul, *One Holy Passion*.

153

For it is God who works in you to will and to do according to his good purpose. (Phil. 2:13)

$\mathcal{Y}$ou'll have trouble believing this next story, but it's true. For many years my father was a general in the U.S. Army. He wasn't the typical image of an army general. He was a "velvet-covered brick"—strong and decisive, but so warm and gracious and encouraging in the process that he came across as if his greatest pleasure was to help his subordinates do their jobs well. Every command he had, officers asked to serve under him.

At the age of eighty-one, Daddy lay in a hospital, dying of stomach cancer. He was weak and thin and in terrible pain, near the end of his long struggle. Then a nurse across the room dropped something. Daddy sprang out of bed and retrieved it for her!

He didn't really mean to do it; he was embarrassed by it and probably exhausted by it. What he did was simply reflex action, the habit of so many years.

Well, "abiding in Christ" can be pictured a lot of ways, but think about the image of my dear daddy in his hospital bed trying to help a nurse far more capable than he. The point is, abide in Christ and *stay there*. For your own good, rest in Him and let Him do His work in you, on you, on your behalf. He doesn't expect you to do it for Him, and you can't, anyway. For you're too weak to do the kind of business that only God can do.

Disciplines of the Heart

"I am the vine, you are the branches. He who abides in Me, and I in him, bears much fruit; for without Me you can do nothing." (John 15:5 NKJV)

Our family used to go to Cape Cod every summer. Many times when the tide was low we looked eyeball to eyeball at some little sea creature in his shell. He wasn't a bit afraid of us; *we* were the ones who were afraid! There we were with all our sixty-nine hundred square inches apiece of exposed skin—and all his possible bites and pinches. But he was safe. He knew, as long as he stayed retracted in that nice, strong shell, that we couldn't get to him.

And as far as all eternity is concerned, you're safe in Christ.

As far as all the hassles of your life are concerned, you're safe in Him.

As far as all your unknowns are concerned, you're safe.

As far as all the world, the flesh and the devil are concerned—*you're safe*.

But what if that little fellow, instead of staying safe in his shell, comes right out and he's sunning himself on our hand, totally unconcerned? Now he's vulnerable to anything, everything.

If you refuse to learn what it means to abide in Christ; if you insist on living out there where you worry and you strive and you're insecure and even disobedient; if you deliberately choose to live as if you were not in Christ at all—you're totally vulnerable, and you're in deep trouble with yourself and with God.

He *commands* you to learn to abide in Him and stay there. He *requires* that you settle down and shelter yourself in Him and trust Him absolutely. He *insists on* your living your life *in Him*, with its resulting rest and joy. If you don't, He loves you too much to neglect you; He'll childtrain you and chastise you until you consciously come *into Him*.

You need the "holy habit" of saying to the Father under any circumstances, "You are my hiding place"—saying it continually, and saying it in peace and stability and joy.

Confident in Christ

*R*emember that God's ways are outside of and above the events of history and time. He doesn't look at the crucifixion as an event that's far away because it happened long ago—and neither must we. Morally and spiritually the cross is equally close to everybody, an ever-present reality.

What does the cross mean to you today?

It's true that Christ died that you might live, but it's also true that He died that you might *die*. This isn't something you *try* to do; your baptism into Him is so complete that when He died, you died.

After Romans 6:3 makes this bold pronouncement that all who were baptized into Christ were baptized into His death, the next verse goes on to make it clear that you went with Him right into the tomb: "We were therefore buried with him" (v. 4). Remember, Jesus didn't just swoon or faint. He actually became dead and was put into a grave. His death was a true death.

Since all that has happened to Him has happened to you, in a very real sense God, the divine Coroner, pronounces you legally dead. That's the absolute, clear-cut end of you—for a new beginning in Christ.

Confident in Christ

Out of the fear and dread of the tomb,
    Jesus, I come, Jesus, I come;
Into the joy and light of Thy home,
    Jesus, I come to Thee.
                                        —W. T. *Sleeper*

*B*efore his conversion Augustine, who became one of the great Christians of the early church, had been quite a rounder. One day he went back to his old neighborhood and one of his former girlfriends saw him and cried, "Augustine! I haven't seen you for so long!"

Augustine began to run from her. The girl called, "Augustine! Don't you remember me? It's I!"

"Yes," Augustine called back, "but I am not I!"

Augustine had died to that old life, and it had no more claim on him. This is exactly what Romans 6 says:

> For we know that our old self was crucified with him so that the body of sin might be rendered powerless, that we should no longer be slaves to sin—because anyone who has died has been freed from sin. (vv. 6–7)

You have a clean break with the past. You're truly emancipated from your old slavery to self. God has made this act so radical, He describes it as death for you. The pre-Christian part of your life is crucified; it's finished; you're dead to sin.

Tell yourself that there is an impassable gulf—a gulf as wide and deep as death—between you and what you once were. "Count yourselves dead to sin" (v. 11).

Confident in Christ

Forgetting what is behind . . . , I press on. (Phil. 3:13, 14)

157

*B*ecause God is a faithful Gardener, you can be sure that now and then He's going to prune His branches. That's what Jesus says in John 15:2: "He cuts off every branch . . . that bears no fruit, while every branch that does bear fruit he prunes [trims clean] so that it will be even more fruitful."

Every branch, sooner or later, is cut by the knife. Pruning cleans up the vine to keep it vital and strong. God trims off anything that will hinder your strength so that you might be fully enabled to produce luscious, beautiful fruit. Through His pruning work, God is training and developing His own.

What does God, the faithful Gardener, trim away from you?

God prunes you of sin. When you first accepted the Lord your concept of sin was superficial, and your trimming could be only superficial and partial. But the more you experience what it is to be "in Christ," the more radical the surgery can be, and the more eager you will be for fully matured fruit in your life.

He will help you cut off the one in order to more fully receive the other. He will help you lose your life to find it. He will help you sell everything to buy the treasure. He will help you to release in order to receive back.

And He will use a very sharp knife.

To be united with Jesus in His death means for the believer a complete and drastic break with sin. His life must reproduce towards sin the implacable hostility which Jesus declared to it by His death.*

Confident in Christ

---

*James S. Stewart, *A Man in Christ.*

We died to sin; how can we live in it any longer?
(*Rom. 6:2*).

A look at an alcoholic helps explain this. Every time he passes a certain bar he stops in and drinks until he's out cold. How is he going to be helped over this? What can ever break his habit?

There's one sure cure: death. When he dies, he'll never drink again. You could run a bottle right under his nose and he wouldn't respond. You could wheel his coffin right by the door of the bar, his friends could all be calling to him—and he'd never move. Alcoholism can follow him only as far as death; then he's free.

When Christ died, you died. Those things that once had a grip on your life had no further right to you. Sin may call you, try to cling to you, but you need no longer be distracted.

"Well," you're saying, "maybe I don't *need* to be distracted by sin, but I *am*!" What we're going to say next is crucial to your faith-life (and it seems is very little followed today).

Don't shape your Christianity from your human observation, experiences, feelings; shape it from God's Word.

God says you are dead to sin (Rom. 6:1–8). And then, knowing we'll question that, He commands us to consider it true: "In the same way, count yourselves dead to sin but alive to God" (v. 11).

Only when you accept what He says will His truth begin to change your life. Then, at last, sin will no longer have the upper hand over you (v. 12), to distract and tempt and hassle you.

The point is to *believe God* when He says you're dead to all that, and you're free.

Confident in Christ

159

γou share His death, says Romans 6:5, because you've been united with Him. It uses a Greek word for *united* that literally means "grown together."

This picture of our being united with Christ in His death makes you think of John 15, where we're called a branch that's been grafted. And there you see a deeper dimension to your identification with Him in death.

When a branch is grafted into a stock on which it's going to grow, both must be cut. There's no grafting without wounding.

The tree must be cut. The inner life of the tree must be opened up and laid bare if it's to receive and take to itself that foreign branch. The branch must be cut, too—cut to fit the cut in the tree, so that the two wounds can be put together with the closest possible fit, and then bound and held there until they receive each other and become one.

The Lord Jesus was wounded and opens Himself up to us fully, saying, "Abide in Me. Stay close, so you can receive My life and My nourishment and all My blessings, and so that the two of us may be perfectly joined."

We can't dictate how it's to happen. We can't say, "I'll come—but I'm the executive type, O Christ. I'll take your blessings, but let me keep my 'self' intact."

No, we must share in "the fellowship of his sufferings, *being conformed to his death*" (Phil. 3:10 NKJV). We must be cut, too—and cut to fit. The cutting involves suffering. Don't think that His is the only sacrifice. "The sufferings of Christ flow over into our lives" (2 Cor. 1:5).

The early Christians rejoiced "because they had been counted worthy of suffering disgrace for the Name" (Acts 5:41).

> O God, to us may grace be giv'n
> To follow in their train!

Confident in Christ.

$\mathcal{W}$e think of *with* as an external word. A physical education teacher says, "Now, do this *with me*," and teacher and student work side by side. So we're apt to pray, *"Lord, be with me."*

But it's not like that with Him. You won't understand "with Christ" until you understand "in Christ." When Romans 6:8 says you died "with Christ," it's not as if you were another thief on a separate cross who died with Him side by side. No! Because you are "in Him" you have common organic functionings. When you graft new skin onto a body, the new skin takes on the rhythms and the metabolism of the body.

This is why, *in Christ*, everything that happened to Him happened to you. You are one *with Him* because you are *in Him.* Living *in Christ* means living out the life of Christ.

God didn't leave His Son hanging on a cross—and neither does He leave you experiencing only being crucified with Him and nothing more: you also are to experience personally, continually, the power of His resurrection life!

> We were . . . buried with him through baptism into death in order that, just as Christ was raised from the dead through the glory of the Father, we too may live a new life.
> If we have been united with him . . . in his death, we will certainly also be united with him in his resurrection. (Rom. 6:4–5)

Wonderful! Every day of your life you're an Easter Christian!

Confident in Christ

> Soar we now where Christ has led: Alleluia!
> Foll'wing our exalted Head: Alleluia!
> Made like Him, like Him we rise: Alleluia!
> Ours the cross, the grave, the skies! Alleluia!
> —*Charles Wesley*

161

*A*t the age of eight our son Nels was playing Little League baseball. In his division that year the winning team was the Padres (six wins and one loss). Their standing was number one; they were the champions. And Nels was *in* the Padres. He was *in* that particular team.

It didn't mean he'd lost his personal identity. He was the only one named Nels Ortlund and he had his own particular function: He played outfielder. And believe me, even though all the little guys wore blue uniforms and caps, you can be sure his parents in the bleachers could pick him out from the rest of the team!

Because Nels was *in* the Padres, he was considered a winner. Because the Padres were champions, Nels was a champion, too. "In" his third grade class or "in" Sunday school he might be something else. But "in" the Padres—no matter how poorly he might play on a given day—he was number one.

So with you, "in" Christ. You may be having a bad day, you may feel down on yourself. But you're identified with a winner—and in Christ you're a winner, too!

> Enclosed in Christ!
> His joy, despite conditions,
> Is always mine.
> His victory is sure.
> In Him we live, and move,
> And have our being.
> His power is boundless,
> And will e'er endure.
>
> *—Mrs. F. McQuat, "Mother Mac," a shut-in member of one of our churches*
>
> *Confident in Christ*

162

$\mathcal{M}$issionary Hudson Taylor in China, after a long period of struggle in his faith, came to write this in a letter:

> The sweetest part . . . is the *rest* which full identification with Him brings. No longer is there need to be anxious about anything, for He, I know, is able to carry out His will, and His will is mine.

In Christ you have great advantages. You're God's personal miracle. You're transferred from the Kingdom of Darkness to the Kingdom of His Son. You're held secure by Him. You're given all the treasures of wisdom and knowledge. You have a solid front line of defense against the Enemy. And you're given fullness in Christ.

Maybe you're saying, "It all seems so intangible, so abstract. It just doesn't excite me."

Let me answer that with an illustration. There was a time when Ray said to me, "I love you. I want you to be my wife." I could have said, "But that seems so intangible—'I love you; I want you to be my wife'!" Except that I read into those words a name, a family, a house, a bank account, a friend, a social escort. It didn't seem at all intangible to me!

God says to us, "I love you, and I want to put you forever into Christ."

And you can read into that . . . everything.

> Thou, O Christ, art all I want;
>   More than all in Thee I find.

Confident in Christ

*F*rom the first three chapters of Ephesians alone, see the advantages you have of being in Christ. You're:

1. Blessed with every spiritual blessing (1:3);

2. Chosen before the creation of the world (1:4);

3. Loved (1:4); 4. Predestined (1:5, 11); 5. Adopted (1:5); 6. Accepted (1:6); 7. Redeemed (1:7); 8. Forgiven (1:7);

9. Lavishly given God's grace (1:7–8; 2:7);

10. Shown the mystery of His will (1:9, 10);

11. Given a guaranteed inheritance (1:11, 14);

12. Made "for the praise of His glory" (1:12);

13. Secured by the Holy Spirit (1:13);

14. Called to a glorious hope (1:18);

15. Made a recipient of God's power (1:19);

16. Made alive together with Christ (2:5);

17. Raised up with Christ (2:6); 18. Seated with Him in the heavenly realms (2:6);

19. Created as God's masterful workmanship, for the purpose of good works (2:10); 20. Brought near to God (2:13);

21. Brought into relationships of peace (2:14);

22. United into one body of Christ (2:15–16; 3:6); made a fellow citizen with God's people (2:19) and a member of His household (2:19);

23. Created for the Spirit's habitation (2:21–22);

24. Made a partaker of God's promises (3:6);

25. Given the revelation of His mysteries (3:8–11); and

26. Given bold and confident access to God (3:12).

Confident in Christ

*B*esides the twenty-six advantages of your new position in Christ listed in Ephesians 1–3, other New Testament references proclaim that in Christ you're:

27. No longer condemned (Rom. 8:29);

28. Made a child of God (John 1:12; 1 John 3:1–2);

29. Foreknown (Rom. 8:29); 30. Called (Rom. 8:30);

31. Justified (Rom. 3:24; 5:1; 8:30); 32. Glorified (Rom. 8:30); 33. Sanctified (1 Cor. 1:30);

34. Made a recipient of eternal life (Rom. 6:23);

35. Made a new creation (2 Cor. 5:17);

36. Reconciled to God (2 Cor. 5:19);

37. Made righteous (2 Cor. 5:21);

38. Made a citizen of heaven (Phil. 3:20);

39. Made complete (Col. 2:10): 40. Made perfect (Heb. 10:14); and 41. Made His own (1 Pet. 2:9).

And there are others! One of our good friends, preaching one time on the blessings we have in Christ, exploded, "We're the hottest commodity this side of the Trinity!"

Once, before Dr. Donald Grey Barnhouse was to preach, a girl sang a beautiful solo, which ended with these words:

> I am satisfied with Jesus. . . .
> But the question comes to me as I think of Calvary:
> Is my Master satisfied with me?

And Dr. Barnhouse came to the pulpit and shouted, "YES, HE IS! You are *in* the Lord Jesus Christ, and God is utterly and eternally satisfied with you!"

Confident in Christ

*B*ow down and worship me," said Satan, taking Jesus to a very high mountain and showing Him all the kingdoms of the world and their splendor, appealing to the lust of the eye. "All this I will give you if you will bow down and worship me" (Matt. 4:8–9).

And with this enticement the devil promised that he would make Christ a world power without the cross and all that suffering. He passed before Jesus' vision the world and all its glory, beauty, strength—all its art, thought, and work. "Worship me, and all you see will be yours," said Satan.

But Jesus wasn't after earthly kingdoms; He was after *the* Kingdom. There could never be His ultimate crown without the cross. He kept His eye on that future! He knew what you and we must always remember: The temporary is no substitute for the eternal. And so "for the joy that was set before Him," He endured and resisted temptation.

Christian, so can you!

You Don't Have to Quit

God's grace teaches us to say

NO

to ungodliness and worldly passions,
and to live
self-controlled, upright and godly lives
in this present age
while we wait for
the blessed hope.
(*Titus 2:12–13*)

*O*ver four hundred years ago Francis de Sales wrote this:

> As soon as you perceive yourself tempted, follow the example of children when they see a wolf or a bear in the country, for they immediately run into the arms of their father or mother. . . .
>
> Run in spirit to embrace the holy cross, as if you saw our Saviour Jesus Christ crucified before you. Protest that you never will consent to the temptation, implore his assistance against it, and still refuse your consent as long as the temptation shall continue.
>
> But . . . *look not the temptation in the face, but look only to our Lord.**

Why? Because every time you fix your eyes on the temptation, you'll be that much weaker and more apt to yield.

When the woman **saw** . . . the fruit of the tree. . . , she **took** . . . it. (Gen. 3:6).

Achan . . . **saw** . . . the plunder. . . . and. . . . **took** them. (Josh. 7:20–21)

David . . . . **saw** a woman . . . . and **took** her. (2 Sam. 11:2, 4 KJV)

Watch, for instance, what you absorb of the daily news. Dirty people love dirt; that's why so much of the news is about dirt. So you, too, take it into your mind, you picture it, you imagine it . . . . Now your own mind is dirty as well. And from a dirty mind spring dirty acts. The news media are powerful transmitters of moral diseases.

This is all-out war. As long as you live, don't let down your guard.

Fix Your Eyes on Jesus

---

*Francis de Sales, *Introduction to a Devout Life*.

*W*e're all a little cuckoo. "All we like sheep have gone astray" (Isa. 53:6 KJV). We all have tendencies to get off course, to major on the minors, to get excited over some lesser doctrine, to put our energies into some passing fad, to stake our last dollar on some quirk, some idiosyncrasy—the shaky and the flaky.

Life is full of land mines! As the Bible says in Ephesians 5:15 (KJV), "See then that ye walk circumspectly"—which means, keep looking around before you put your foot down. There's a lot of the shaky and the flaky around you.

What are some specific things you might steer clear of? Well, here are two, for starters:

1. Beware of public movements that stem from fear. In the early 1960s, fear drove multitudes of Christians in America into such a panic over Communism that many Christian leaders were suddenly suspect. Huge "Christian" rallies were held to alert people to the danger, and they got believers everywhere playing detective, sniffing under every bush and tree to ferret out pastors who might be part of the plot to turn us over to the Russians. Many innocent pastors were hurt.

2. Beware of financial temptations. The best way to get money is still payday by payday. As Proverbs 13:11 says, "He who gathers money little by little makes it grow."

There's a lot of the shaky and the flaky in financial deals.

"Continue to do good," says 1 Peter. Stay married (if you are). Avoid doctrinal excesses. Keep your living honest and careful.

Don't be cuckoo!

Never buy a portable TV set on a sidewalk from a man who's out of breath.

You Don't Have to Quit

*S*atan will come after you in the fiercest temptations. He'll attack you in your three areas of weakness (1 John 2:16):

1. *The lust or the cravings of the flesh:* sexual immorality, overeating, addictive habits, laziness . . .

2. *The lust or the cravings of your eyes:* excessive desires for beauty of any kind—cars, interior decorating, clothes, persons of the opposite sex . . .

3. *The pride of life:* overgrown appetites for money, status, or power, which lead to jealousy, slander, cheating, and "every form of malice" (Eph. 4:31).

Why does Satan hassle you, says A. W. Tozer?

A Christian is a constant threat to the stability of Satan's government. The Christian is a holy rebel loose in the world with access to the throne of God. Satan never knows from what direction the danger will come.

Who knows when another Elijah will arise, or another Daniel? or a Luther or a Booth?

Who knows when an Edwards or a Finney may go in and liberate a whole town or countryside by the preaching of the Word and prayer?

Such a danger is too great to tolerate, so Satan gets to the new convert as early as possible to prevent his becoming too formidable a foe.*

Oh, my friend, thwart Satan's desires for you, and surrender yourself to become a great power for God!

You Don't Have to Quit

---

*"The Editorial Voice," *The Alliance Weekly,* 6 March 1963.

God doesn't cause your temptations, but He does allow them.

> When tempted, no one should say, "God is tempting me." . . . Each one is tempted when, by his own evil desire, he is dragged away and enticed. (James 1:13–14)

Be careful about that old saw, "You can't keep the birds from landing on your head—just don't let them build a nest in your hair." We use it to say, "It's no big deal if I'm tempted. Jesus was tempted, too."

Listen, you're not Jesus! *Flap your arms!* When they see your head or mine, they're positively *tempted* to land on us! These proverbial buzzards see inside of us our "evil desire," as James says, and they chirp, "Come on, everybody, that sucker's an easy touch. We can settle in there for sure." Then, as James goes on to say, the evil desire leads to sin, and the sin leads to death!

And it all began with what we thought was a harmless little temptation.

But here's the good news: *You don't have to yield.*

> God is faithful; he will not let you be tempted beyond what you can bear. But when you are tempted, he will also provide a way out so that you can stand up under it. (1 Cor. 10:13)

> Because [Jesus] himself suffered when he was tempted, he is able to help those who are being tempted. (Heb. 2:18)

So what do you do when you're tempted? **You fix your eyes not on the temptation, but on Jesus.** Then you'll "find grace to help . . . in [your] time of need" (Heb. 4:16).

Fix Your Eyes on Jesus

*I*f you're in a troubled time of life, there are three possibilities for your future.

One, God is just about to change your bad situation. There was the apostle Peter in prison—in perfect trust, asleep! Suddenly an angel got him up and led him to freedom (see Acts 12:3–11). Just like that.

Two, He'll change your situation later, but not yet. Lazarus, Jesus' dear friend, was dying. His sisters rushed Jesus the news. But Jesus lingered where He was two more days—indeed, letting Lazarus die (see John 11:6). His perfect plan wasn't to heal a sick man, but to raise a dead one.

God's timing is right. One of the most often-repeated commands in the Bible is to "wait on the Lord." Waiting on Him "grows you up"; it keeps your eyes off yourself and on Him; it gives you staying power.

Three, He doesn't plan to change your bad situation ever, as long as you live. Now, that's tough! How could God do that to you?

The apostle John was exiled to the Island of Patmos. He could have spent his time pacing that barren little beach, feeling bitter about what "they" did to him, and scanning the horizon every minute for a rescuer. But he didn't.

Quieted under the hand of God into a position of trust and receptivity, John received the most fabulous revelation of Jesus Christ and His future that any man has ever received, and as a result he wrote the Spirit-breathed book of Revelation.

Do you feel as if you're on a "Patmos" in your life? Are you feeling caught and trapped? Settle down. Look up. Let God decide whether He will act according to One, Two, or Three. For you, it will be perfect.

You Don't Have to Quit

171

Do not be anxious about anything, but in everything, by prayer and petition, with thanksgiving, present your requests to God. And the peace of God, which transcends all understanding, will guard your hearts and your minds in Christ Jesus. (Phil. 4:6–7)

Worry is unnecessary.
    The Lord is looking out for you and yours.
Worry is futile.
    It never solves the problem.
Worry is harmful.
    Doctors agree it causes many health problems.
Worry is sin.
    It doubts the wisdom and love and power of
        God.

*D*o you believe in the sun even when it isn't shining? Then believe in God even when He seems silent.

Faith in God
    sees the invisible,
    believes the incredible,
    and receives the impossible.

For your life . . .

Grace, mercy and peace from God the Father and Christ Jesus our Lord. (2 Tim. 1:2)

Grace for every step,
Mercy for every stumble,
Peace for every situation.

YOU HAVE A MAGNIFICENT VIEW—
IF YOU LOOK STRAIGHT UP.

Disciplines of the Home

Suppose right now you hit your hand really hard on something sturdy nearby.

Does it hurt?

"Boy," you say, "that really stings."

Wait a minute. Does it still hurt?

"Yes," you say, "I can still feel it."

Think about that hurt. Concentrate on it. If you do, you'll feel it for quite a while.

Now what if you saw your only little daughter out in the street just about to get run over by a car, and in the nick of time you grabbed her from the car's path, but in so doing you hit your hand—as hard as you hit it just now.

Would it hurt?

You're smiling. "I wouldn't even be aware of it," you say, "I'd be so thrilled that my daughter was safe."

Exactly.

Living is between your ears. You can develop your own high pain threshold by concentrating on what's important and wonderful. Look not at your pain, but at your progress.

Paul said about his hardships,

> But *none of these things move me*, neither count I my life dear unto myself, so that I might finish my course with joy, and the ministry, which I have received of the Lord Jesus, to testify the gospel of the grace of God. (Acts 20:24 KJV, emphasis added)

You're no martyr when you ignore pain to choose the joy of exciting accomplishment! That's *learning how to be hurt.*

You Don't Have to Quit

Cast all your anxiety on [the Lord] because he cares for you" (1 Pet. 5:7). He takes the responsibility. You can "loose up"!

Note that word *all* in that verse. Sometimes we can get hung up on just one problem.

I know a pastor's wife who functioned beautifully through the years until her daughter became a rebel and married poorly. Then this woman took this care upon herself. And she went into such grieving that for the rest of her life she was disconsolate. She was a poor wife, a burden to her friends, a discredit to God. Her entire mental focus was on the disgrace of her daughter.

Cast on Him all your anxieties—every one. And what if they come back into your mind? Cast them on Him again, and keep casting them on Him as often as you need to. Tell Him, "Lord, I can't carry this burden. You carry it for me. And let's make a deal: I'll take Your peace instead!" (See John 14:27.)

But then, what if the thing you fear the very most of all happens to you? What if God does to you what He did to Shadrach, Meshach, and Abednego—throws you into a fiery furnace?

The basic truth is that God is good, and He loves you to the end, and your reasonable expectation is that He'll give you what you hope for in your life. But *"even if he does not"* (Dan. 3:18)— He is still good, and He is still in charge. He will still take care of you.

You can even experience a holy, happy carelessness!

You can "loose up"!

Disciplines of the Heart

PRAYER OF SAINT PATRICK

I establish myself today in:
    The power of God to guide me,
    The might of God to uphold me,
    The wisdom of God to teach me,
    The eye of God to watch over me,
    The ear of God to hear me,
    The word of God to speak to me,
    The hand of God to protect me,
    The way of God to lie before me,
    The shield of God to shelter me,
    The hosts of God to defend me.

Christ with me, Christ before me,
Christ behind me, Christ within me,
Christ beneath me, Christ above me,
Christ at my right, Christ at my left,
Christ in breadth, Christ in length,
Christ in height, Christ in the heart
    of every man who thinks of me,
Christ in the mouth of every man
    who speaks to me,
Christ in the ear of every man
    who hears me.

Confident in Christ

God has the right to prune you of your natural talents and abilities.

At first that seems silly. When we accept Christ, shouldn't we start exercising our natural gifts for Him?

But everything we have, in ourselves, is still defiled by sin and under the influence of the flesh. We know how religious people can rise to great prominence and then be exposed as "Elmer Gantrys," using their natural abilities for their own corrupt ends.

God has the right to cut away all that we can do in ourselves. We must surrender to let Him do it, if He desires. Then what He leaves *is surrendered to Him;* it's His property, bearing His stamp and revealing His influence, and used only under His total control. Not only your natural talents and abilities, but even your spiritual gifts must be laid humbly on the altar at Jesus' feet.

In this age of narcissism some Christians are pouncing on spiritual gifts in an over-emphasis on self-analyses and testings and comparisons. Says Theodore Monod, "You must not gloat over your gifts, counting them like treasures, but spend them immediately and remain poor, 'looking unto Jesus.'"

As soon as you begin to get self-satisfied in the possessions of spiritual gifts, the "inflow of grace is retarded," as Andrew Murray says, and stagnation threatens.

Stay centered on Christ! Stay humble! Stay amazed at what He's given, and eager to give it back to Him! Let the flow be two-way and full of love.

This is abiding in Christ.

Confident in Christ

1. *An eye fixed on self is full of confusion:* How much commitment is commitment? If I teach a Sunday school class, can I never go away weekends? If I join the choir, what happens when choir practice night comes and I'm exhausted?

The "me generation" says, "I can only be somewhat committed to you because I'm first committed to me."

> [A man] said, "I will follow you, Lord; but first let me go back and say good-by to my family."
> Jesus replied, "No one who puts his hand to the plow and looks back is fit for service in the kingdom of God." (Luke 9:61–62)

But fix your eyes on Jesus, and you yourself will be helped the most.

2. *An eye fixed on service to others is full of politics,* and the service is performed in

> bossiness,
>
> fussiness,
>
> competition,
>
> criticalness,
>
> self-will,
>
> ego.

But fix your eyes on Jesus, and others will be helped the most.

Are you a "ministry-centered" person? You'll get depleted, irritated, abrasive, and exhausted.

Are you a "Christ-centered" person? Even as you serve Him, you'll stay nourished, happy, rested.

Fix Your Eyes on Jesus

$\mathcal{N}$arcissus, in Greek mythology, pined away to almost nothing for love of his own reflection in water—and so do Christians who catch his disease.

We live in a narcissistic age—even within Christianity. Many of us believers have an excessive interest in—and affection for—

> ourselves, our feelings,
>
> our relationships, our abilities,
>
> our lifestyles,
>
> our spiritual development,
>
> our knowledge, our growth,
>
> our maturity—

anything involving *us!* So for the last few years, studying spiritual gifts has been a "natural"—complete with personality testings.

The Holy Spirit gives gifts not for us but for others:

> Each one should use whatever gift he has received to serve others, faithfully administering God's grace in its various forms. (1 Pet. 4:10)

Yesterday's grace passed with yesterday's service. Today's grace is only for today. Gifts are bestowed for each situation's need in the body, and they're not given to look at but *to use*.

Says Theodore Monod, "We are not to gloat over [our gifts] as treasures, counting up our riches, but to spend them immediately and remain poor, 'looking unto Jesus.'"

Fix Your Eyes on Jesus

$\mathcal{E}$go can get us in the habit of feeling accountable for all the ills of the world! We can try to carry a load that only God can bear—to feel guilty over all the pain and injustice on our planet, to groan under the weight, and to think it all wouldn't happen if only we would "do" something.

The late Pope John was once begged by a very concerned cardinal to relieve the problems of the world. The story has it that Pope John put his arm around the cardinal and said he'd been helped recently by a dream he'd had. He said in his dream an angel came into the papal bedroom and said, "Hey, there, Johnny boy, don't take yourself so seriously."

Understand God's side, understand our side! His side is to let sin play itself out to the end of its rope and then to come in mighty judgment and set the world right. Our side is to pray, to give, to serve and help to the uttermost as He guides us—but still to hug to our hearts the secret knowledge of the sovereignty of God. He is at work. He knows.

In the big picture, all is well.
We trust Him.
We rest in Him.

Disciplines of the Heart

Then the sovereignty, power and greatness of the kingdoms under the whole heaven will be handed over to the saints, the people of the Most High. His kingdom will be an everlasting kingdom, and all rulers will worship and obey him. (Dan. 7:27)

*L*ove is not self-seeking" (1 Cor. 13:5). It's fulfilled in helping others.

I sat in a Bible conference once, listening to a missionary doctor from Africa. He told of driving a jeep all one night to take a woman back from the hospital to the village where she lived. There didn't seem to be anyone else to do it, and she had to go home, so he took her. The rain never let up once during that long, dark night, during that entire round trip, and part of the way the roads were almost impossible.

By the time he got back it was dawn. He was soaked, muddied, exhausted. He showered and went to work. Nobody at the hospital all day thanked him, nobody commended him, and this doctor simply had to pray, "Lord, that trip was for You. I'm glad the woman could get home, but I really did it for You, and Your commendation is enough."

When we go to our daily round of tasks in life, we go as servants. We don't protect ourselves. For us, God's commendation is enough.

"Love is not self-seeking."

Disciplines of the Home

We who are strong ought to bear with the failings of the weak and not to please ourselves. Each of us should please his neighbor for his good, to build him up. For even Christ did not please himself. (Rom. 15:1–3)

So we make it our goal to please him. (2 Cor. 5:9)

*N*ever mind the features and figure you were born with,"
says 1 Peter. "What will adorn you with an illusion of beauty is
a meek and quiet spirit, which is precious in the sight of God."

In other words, the beautiful woman is disciplined, chaste,
discreet, deferring, gracious, controlled, "together." This kind of
woman God considers godly, which means she's got His qualities, and she's close to His heart. This is "His kind of woman"!—
His kind of beautiful woman.

Now, under this umbrella of characteristics, she can have
all kinds of personalities and still be beautiful. She can be viva-
cious or shy, colorful or cool, an administrator or a follower. She
can be a corporation president or she can bake delicious molas-
ses cookies—or both.

When a woman has God's beauty—a meek and quiet
spirit—she isn't threatening to those around her. She doesn't
compete; she doesn't "demand her rights," because she's secure.
Her trust is in God to exalt her in His own way and time, and
He does! He can afford to expand her gifts and increase her
place in the world, because she's not grasping for it. That's
God's kind of beautiful woman.

Disciplines of the Beautiful Woman

> She is clothed with strength and dignity;
> > she can laugh at days to come.
> She speaks with wisdom,
> > and faithful instruction is on her tongue. . . .
> Charm is deceptive, and beauty is fleeting;
> > but a woman who fears the LORD is to be
> > > praised.

(Prov. 31:25–26, 30)

181

Suddenly—really since World War II—our role as women is drastically changing. I see our greatest danger not in the new things we're stepping out and doing, but in the areas which as a consequence we're neglecting.

Titus 2:3–5 commands the younger women

To love their husbands and children,

> To be self-controlled and pure,
>
> To be busy at home,
>
> To be kind, and
>
> To be subject to their husbands.

In these darkening "last days,"

> Too many husbands and children are not loved.
>
> Too many women are no longer "self-controlled and pure, . . . busy at home, . . . kind, . . . subject to their husbands."

And, remembering 1 Timothy 5:10,

> Children are often not being truly "brought up."
>
> Hospitality has dwindled.
>
> Practical needs are not always being met.
>
> Those in trouble are often neglected.
>
> All kinds of "good deeds" frequently don't get done.

And citizens put more and more pressure on the government to meet these needs—because so many women have shifted to paying jobs and are no longer taking care of them.

Such a drastic change demands a drastic rethinking.

We must remember our original calling to be women.

Whatever the sacrifice, we must get back to the basics, to what God has called us to be and do as women—which only we, and nobody else, can be and do.

Disciplines of the Home

182

Says our heavenly Father in statements that are blatantly sexist,

> Adam was formed first, then Eve. (1 Tim. 2:13)
>
> The head of the woman is man. (1 Cor. 11:3)

To praise, enjoy, be comfortable with, and, yes, follow these guys in our lives has got to be a voluntary thing. "You first, honey . . . You first, my brother." Easy or not, it must initiate with us women.

Will this attitude produce insipid doormats? Yes, it will and often does—in vast areas of the world where it's merely a cultural tradition. And then enormous reservoirs of brains and gifts are wasted and lost.

But if a woman's "you first" is a spiritual decision, then it's simply saying that God calls the shots. In that case, one of two things will happen.

One, she'll learn to follow with grace and poise. And, generally speaking, she'll be honored and elevated and her gifts fulfilled in every way, because her unthreatening, encouraging attitude will evoke a similar response in the males.

Or two, the Lord may sovereignly choose to set aside the rules and appoint her a judge like Deborah, or a prophetess like one of Philip's daughters, or a corporation president, or who knows what.

She'll be ready for whatever God plans.

Disciplines of the Home

*W*hat does the Bible have to say about a family's lifestyle? It certainly doesn't say women can't work. Lydia was a dealer in expensive purple fabric (Acts 16:14). Aquila and Priscilla were a married couple in business together (Acts 18:3). Dorcas was a dressmaker—although maybe not for salary (Acts 9:36, 39). The woman of Proverbs 31 bought and sold property and clothing and who knows what else (vv. 13–27).

But the Bible has everything to say about seeking first God's kingdom. It has strong words about not letting concern for food and clothes get in the way of following His principles (Matt. 6:25–33).

It says to be a family of enthusiasts for God and for His Word! Whatever it costs doesn't matter. It says, keep your eyes on Him, on His plans for your lives, and on the jolly good fun of carrying out those plans.

Henry Ford once said,

> You can do anything if you have enthusiasm. Enthusiasm is the yeast that makes your hopes rise to the stars. Enthusiasm is the sparkle in your eyes, the swing in your gait, the grip of your hand, the irresistible surge of will and energy to execute your ideas.
>
> Enthusiasts are fighters. They have fortitude. They have staying qualities. Enthusiasm is at the bottom of all progress. With it, there is accomplishment. Without it, there are only alibis.

Enthusiasts *are fighters*. They don't let their lives just go with the flow. Enthusiasts *have fortitude*. They're willing to be separate from all that is cheap, vulgar, desensitizing, degrading.

Enthusiasts *have staying power*. They maintain godly habits which, over the long haul, build them into winners.

Disciplines of the Home

God's beautiful women have been used even in mass spiritual turnings that have affected whole nations and generations. If you're a woman reading this—one of my sisters—you're an important key to revival in our day.

When Paul heard the call to come to Europe for the first time and preach the gospel there, he traveled to Philippi, a key center, and found his way to a group of key women holding a prayer meeting (Acts 16:13). From this small but strategic group, Christianity spread out until the whole known world was affected by it.

Through the centuries, God's beautiful women with "gentle and quiet spirits" (1 Pet. 3:4) have suffered hardships, rocked cradles, and—you know the rest.

God's longest description of his ideal woman, in Proverbs 31, ends with these words: "These good deeds of hers shall bring her honor and recognition from people of importance" (Prov. 31:31 TLB).

In recent years we have been obsessed with figuring out what a woman should be allowed to do. God says in His Word a woman can do anything; the point is not what she *does* but what she *is*. When a women is wise, and full of kind words, and hard-working and conscientious, and helpful to her man if she has one, and deeply reverent in her love for God—in other words, if she is a "beautiful woman"—she can do anything in this whole wide world.

But with all this God-given, legitimate power, how do we as women influence the world for God? By influencing our *personal* worlds to Him. And how do we do that? By returning to Him first ourselves, with all our hearts. Will it be easy? Of course not. The worthwhile, the best, never is. It will include disciplines—daily disciplines, to change us and change those around us.

If you're a housewife with little ones underfoot, don't chafe! This is not only their training ground, it's yours.

Disciplines of the Beautiful Woman

Now Moses was tending the flock of Jethro his father-in-law. (Exod. 3:1)

*D*o you feel as if nothing of significance is happening in your life?

I guess so does a lobster, encased in that ridiculous armor. As he grows it even gets crowded inside. But he sheds it fourteen times during his first year of life. Each shedding takes ten days, and each time in the period between shells—when he's naked, exposed, vulnerable—he grows about seven percent.

You feel stifled, unfulfilled? You don't know when you'll break out into change?

Wait for God.

Wait on God.

Wait in God.

Wait with God.

Life is not fixed. Let it happen; don't rush it.

"It is God who works in you to will and to act according to his good purpose. Do everything without complaining or arguing" (Phil. 2:13–14).

Keep your eyes fixed on Him, live in obedience as you see it, and then just wait.

All you're doing is tending sheep, . . . binding up a scratch, . . . leading to a drink of water, . . .

Year after year after year . . .

And then suddenly you notice nearby there's a bush on fire.

Disciplines of the Home

Jesus said to them, "My Father is always at his work to this
very day, and I, too, am working." (John 5:17)

God is at work in all your kaleidoscoping transitions: not
only in the high points but in the endings, beginnings, detours,
dead ends, and in-between times. His powerful tools are not just
the promotions and graduations but the failures and firings and
losses and sicknesses and shocks and periods of boredom. In it
all He's silently, busily, unceasingly encouraging, punishing,
shaping.

"The counselor talked to me, and I think I'll take algebra."
"I can't believe I'm pregnant! What went wrong?"
"I did it! I left teaching to go to seminary."
"I do believe I'm losing some hair, right there on top in
back. I found it in the mirror."
"The doctor says it's cancer."

In them all, God is tenderly, strongly at work.

"In his heart a man plans his course, but the Lord deter-
mines his steps" (Prov. 16:9).

And during all His working—during all God's silent activity in the disappointments, surprises, delights, irritations—
transformations are taking place.

"Lord, Thou art the journey and the journey's end."

Disciplines of the Heart

187

Υour family—whatever the combination of humans under your roof—is a mystery, a marvel, a wonder. God has put you together, and things are happening in you and between you, from day to day, of which you're totally unaware.

His movements are constant, but they're often subdued, delicate, even invisible. Mostly you can only realize what He's been up to in you and your family in retrospect, as you look back. You have to read God's work in your life like Hebrew: backward.

But imperceptibly He's always at it. Don't draw conclusions too quickly about what he's doing. Michel de Montaigne (1533–1592) said, "We undo ourselves by impatience," and he was right. Or as Yogi Berra said, "It isn't over 'til it's over."

God is powerfully at work. Believe what you cannot see; His movements are simply imperceptible to your naked eye.

> The LORD works out everything for his own ends—
> even the wicked for a day of disaster. (Prov. 16:4)

Sometimes Ray and I lead cruises. Each day aboard we get our shoes out of the same closet, our clothes out of the same drawers, and it looks as though nothing has changed. But we're not in the same place! The ship has moved, and we're in brand new waters.

In your life you really never repeat anything. You may use the same words or motions, but you can't repeat an experience, because God has brought you to a new place. Behind the scenes, unnoticed, He's been moving you to where you're never been before. All things are new. Your life isn't cyclical but linear.

Professor Albert Einstein used to clap his hands rapidly twice and say to his students, "Between those two claps, you and I moved thirty miles through space."

Disciplines of the Home

188

$\mathcal{W}$hen you get going in a project and problems crop up, don't assume the project is wrong. Develop an attitude of patience. God is at work backstage.

Jesus told about a fellow whose fig tree hadn't borne any figs for three years, so he told his gardener to cut it down. (That's the latest thinking: If something isn't "working for you," junk it.)

But the gardener was like God—long-suffering before the final judgment! "'Sir,' [he] replied, 'leave it alone for one more year, and I'll dig around it and fertilize it. If it bears fruit next year, fine! If not, then cut it down'" (Luke 13:6–9).

In other words, don't be hasty; don't quit too soon; what a shame if you destroy something that was going to get good.

Almost everything that's terrific today, earlier wasn't.
Any marriage.
Any church.
Any business.
Any person!
Any grape. Tomato. You name it.
Good things take time before they're good.

You Don't Have to Quit

Then they cried to the LORD in their trouble,
    and he saved them from their distress. (Ps. 107:13)

189

$\mathcal{F}$rom here to there, and then from there
        to here
The people of this planet circling roam,
And I, as well—but, oh, one truth is clear:
I live in God, and God Himself is Home.

From hither and from thither comes the call,
Perhaps to places near, perhaps abroad,
But anywhere I am, and through it all
My heart's at home—for Home is Sovereign
        God.

To hurry here, and then to scurry there
May be the thing that duty asks of me;
But oh! my heart is tranquil anywhere,
When God Himself is my Tranquility.

Yes, in my heart of heart *Shekinah* dwells
The Glorious One, the Highest and the Best;
And deep within, I hear cathedral bells
That call me to devotion and to rest.*
          —Anne Ortlund

        Disciplines of the Beautiful Woman

---

*© Copyright 1972.

*W*hy do so many Christians live grey, struggling, carnal lives?

Because they haven't comprehended the vastness of the power within them and what to do with it.

"Well, what *are* we to do with it?" you're asking.

And I answer, "Nothing."

"What?" you squawk. "That's crazy. Of course we're to do something. We have to do something to take advantage of all that power."

A woodpecker was once pecking away on a great tree. Suddenly a huge bolt of lightning struck the tree and with enormous noise and force split it right down the middle, straight to its very roots.

The poor little woodpecker found himself on the ground nearby, half-dead, his feathers torn and singed. And when he gathered himself together he croaked, "I didn't know I could do it!"

So God desires to show His great power in our lives, and we croak, "Now, what shall I do? I certainly have to do something to make this happen."

The answer is really "Stand back!" It's "Take God seriously! Accept His enormous power in your life! Believe it, and be ready for miracles!"

"What must I do," asked the Philippian jailer, "to be saved?"

And Paul answered, "Believe. Just believe, and you'll be saved—that's all it takes. Don't 'do'; you'll just get in the way. Let God do the 'doing'!"

Disciplines of the Heart

What must I do," asked the Philippian jailer, "to be saved?"

And Paul answered, "Believe. Just believe, and you'll be saved—that's all it takes. Don't 'do'; you'll just get in the way. Let God do the 'doing'!"

And that night, as the jailer simply "[came] to believe in God" (Acts 16:34), the Lord God Almighty mysteriously reached down out of eternity and chose him, applied the eternal work of the Cross to that man's account, wrote his name in the Lamb's book of life, washed him of his sins, caused him to be born into His heavenly family, breathed into him eternal life, removed all condemnation from him, deposited in him His Holy Spirit as a "down payment" of more to come, bestowed on him all the riches of His grace, eternally predestined him to be conformed to the image of His Son, made him a co-heir with Christ of all things, called him, justified him, sanctified him, glorified him—and so much more that it will take all eternity for that jailer to discover what God "did" the instant he believed!

When we're itchy to "do," it's usually because we really *don't believe,* so we're trying to help God out. In Jesus' hometown, "he did not do many miracles there because of their lack of faith" (Matt. 13:58). They didn't take seriously His supernatural power so available for them, so He didn't use it! And when we don't understand His resurrection power within us, we develop an activist religion that crowds out the possibility of that giant, explosive power's working in our lives.

Disciplines of the Heart

And this is his command: to believe in the name of his Son, Jesus Christ. (1 John 3:23)

*T*here is God's side and there is our side. The work, the accomplishment, is only His. You in yourself can't be holy and happy, but Christ *can* be—in you and through you—and He will be if you ask Him to and let Him.

"The LORD will accomplish what concerns me" (Ps. 138:8 NASB).

He establishes "the work of our hands" (Ps. 90:17)—our hands, His establishing.

Said Isaiah to the Lord, "All that we have accomplished you have done for us" (Isa. 26:12).

Here's a glove, empty and limp. I hold it up by its wrist and it can't wave, it can't pick up anything, it's helpless. Then I slide my hand into the glove, and my fingers fill all its fingers. Then it can seem full of dexterity and power!

"My, what a wonderful glove!" someone says. "It's so clever and gifted! It's brilliant!"

No, the glove is helpless in itself; it's the hand inside that's brilliant. And you know what? Any old out-of-fashion, funny-looking glove will do!

Your part is to relax and let Him work in you; His part is to achieve fabulous goals in you and for you.

> He who trusts in himself is a fool, but he who walks in
> wisdom [in Christ] is kept safe (Prov. 28:26).

Disciplines of the Heart

*G*rey Christians carve up their lives into "sacred" and "secular." They have an impression that prayer, Bible reading, church attendance, and "fellowship" are sacred acts that make God happy. Then there's eating, sleeping, lovemaking, working, recreation, and all the rest that are secular acts. For these they sort of apologize to God and look on them as necessary waste. And the upshot is that they feel uneasy most of the time and consider themselves "basically secular" Christians.

But the dogged, can't-get-away-from-it fact is that they're Christians—so they have to keep crossing back and forth all their lives between sacred and secular. And their inner hearts tend to break up into dividedness, purposelessness, frustration.

Says A. W. Tozer,

> They try to walk the tight rope between two kingdoms, and they find no peace in either. Their strength is reduced, their outlook is confused and their joy is taken from them.*

Oh, my friend! It is radical and revolutionary and cleansing and purifying for you to see that *God is at work in everything*—and then adjust your life accordingly!

Jesus did. He'd given His whole human life to the Father (Heb. 10:5, 7), and the Father made no distinction between act and act. Jesus ate, He preached, He went to parties, He did miracles, He rested—and He said, "I always do what pleases him" (John 8:29).

"In all thy ways acknowledge him [in memorizing Scripture, in giving yourself a pedicure], and he shall direct thy paths" (Prov. 3:6 KJV). He will enjoy everything you do (and you will enjoy everything He does!) as you live in Him, and He in you.

Disciplines of the Heart

---

*A. W. Tozer, *The Pursuit of God*.

*J*oseph in the book of Genesis is a beautiful model of the maturing Christian. Looking at him, you see what's needed between the womb and adulthood: to learn not to look back but forward, to move from fantasizing to realism; to emerge from being cared for to caring, from being parented to parenting; to gain the courage to be realistic, to adjust, suffer, and achieve.

In other words, *you move from fears to faith.*

In the end a mature, successful Joseph could see the Big Picture and discern through good and through bad the quiet, persistent actions of a loving God. So he could say with total compassion to his chagrined older brothers, "You intended to harm me, but God intended it for good to accomplish what is now being done, the saving of many lives" (Gen. 50:20).

Joseph had come to see eternal truth—that God's reality is infinitely better than all our fantasies, that the losses from leaving the womb really do open up enormous opportunities for gain, that forward is truly better than back, that with God the best wine is always last.

What a joy, then, for you to learn to walk strongly forward with your Abba Father, the Lord God Almighty!

Disciplines of the Home

My life verse: "The path of the just is like the shining sun, that shines ever brighter unto the perfect day" (Prov. 4:18 NKJV).

$\mathcal{T}$he LORD replied, "My Presence will go with you, and I will give you rest."

Then Moses said to him, "If your Presence does not go with us, do not send us up from here." . . .

And the LORD said to Moses, "I will do the very thing you have asked, because I am pleased with you and I know you by name."

Then Moses said, "Now show me your glory."

And the LORD said, "I will cause all my goodness to pass in front of you, and I will proclaim my name, the LORD, in your presence." (Exod. 33:14–15, 17–19)

O Lord, I need to know that You are You!
I need to have a glorious God in view;
To see Your plans, so infinite and wise,
I need a mighty God before my eyes.
     Show me Your glory! Show Yourself anew;
     Lord, open up my eyes of faith to You.

So often, when I face which way to go
The problems seem to multiply and grow;
I do not see you standing, waiting, there,
So full of power for me, to do, to dare!
     Show me Your glory! Show Yourself anew;
     Lord, open up my eyes of faith to You.

O God, I know that in my present state
I could not stand the sight of You, so great;
Yet even now, the smallest glimpse is bright
Enough to bathe my soul in dazzling light!
     Show me your glory! Show yourself anew;
     Lord, open up my eyes of faith to you.

—Anne Ortlund
Women's Devotional Bible

Open your eyes, my friend, and fill all your life with the brightness of the splendor of God! Live all your life seeing your powerful, loving Lord at work everywhere, in everything, in all your circumstances, in all your moments. Psalm 119:91 says, "All things serve [him]." Romans 11:36 says that "From him and through him and to him are all things."

Then nothing—nothing—is without God's wonderful meaning in it. "The earth is the LORD's, and everything in it" (Ps. 24:1). "The whole earth is full of his glory" (Isa. 6:3)! He knows when every sparrow falls, and He knows even the number of the hairs on your head (Matt. 10:29–30). He has established all governments (Rom. 13:1), and the hearts of all governmental rulers are in His hand, doing what He pleases (Prov. 21:1).

If God is truly at work in everything, you have brand new ground rules for living your Christian life.

Literally,

You're to cast all your anxiety on Him because He cares for you (1 Pet. 5:7).

You're not to repay anyone evil for evil; "'I will repay,' says the Lord" (Rom. 12:17–19).

You're not to fear anything, because He's with you (Ps. 23:4).

You'll never lack anything, because He's your Shepherd (Ps. 23:1).

When you pass through hard times, He'll see that they don't get the better of you (Isa. 43:2).

Only if this is true does 1 Thessalonians 5:18 make sense: "Give thanks in all circumstances, for this is God's will for you in Christ Jesus."

Disciplines of the Heart

Let us throw off everything that hinders. (Heb. 12:1)

A little girl was looking at Michelangelo's statue of David, and she said in wonder to the great sculptor, "How did you know he was in there?"

People who learn to visualize see Davids in rocks. Michelangelo needed a mental picture of David before he knew what to cut away.

And the more is cut away, the more important is what remains! The rock that's left is becoming a David!

What we're trying to say is this: when you've pared away superfluous areas from your life (and only you and God will know what they are), the remaining activities must be right. Your life will be increasingly precious, and how you spend it, increasingly important. Isn't that exciting and wonderful?

Only one life—
'Twill soon be past.
Only what's done
For Christ will last.

You Don't Have to Quit

*I*n all your personal trials remember the life of Joseph, and see that in the worst of his situations, his trust in God colored everything.

Jacob's paternal favoritism of Joseph was not good. Joseph's brothers' schemes were not good. Potiphar was not good, prison was not good, famine was not good. But for Joseph and his family, God took a whole string of not-goods and turned them into good (Gen. 50:20; Rom. 8:28). And that is His consistent, eternal way.

Then as you walk through all the traumas of your life, *calmly trust Him.* Keep daily nourished in Scripture and prayer, and *calmly trust Him.* Fix your eyes on Jesus, and *calmly trust Him.*

"Our Lord God Almighty reigns" (Rev. 19:6).

"The LORD God is a sun and shield" (Ps. 84:11).

"Those who are with us are more than those who are with them" (2 Kings 6:16).

"Don't be afraid; just believe" (Mark 5:36).

Faith justifies the soul (Rom. 5:1). It purifies the heart (Acts 15:9). It overcomes the world (1 John 5:4).

In every problem, spell out your needs to Jesus and ask for help. And then—"Stop doubting and believe," as Jesus said (John 20:27). Hope in God for your situations! "Be of good cheer,"—because you have Him!

Let me say it strongly: A doubting, worrying Christian does a lot of harm. He's modeling fear, not faith; and he'll produce other doubting, worrying Christians who have no idea that "God is our refuge and strength, an ever present help in trouble" (Ps. 46:1).

This is of top importance, because "without faith it is impossible to please God" (Heb. 11:6).

Disciplines of the Home

199

*A*biding in Christ is not a self-improvement scheme. If you seek God just to become a better Christian, you've missed the whole point. This isn't for you, it's for Him. This is to dwell in Him, to settle down in Him, to make Him your most familiar surroundings—to abide in Him (John 15: 4, 5), to abide in His love (verses 9 and 10), to give Him glory and pleasure.

And this is not a one-time commitment, it's a daily one. It calls you from all double-mindedness to single-mindedness.

Now let us tell you something wonderful. God began a process at your new birth which is irreversible. Like it or not, kick and scream if you will, if you're a true believer, "He who began a good work in you will carry it on to completion until the day of Christ Jesus" (Philippians 1:6).

If you saw a tadpole when he's half frog, you wouldn't say he's a hypocrite, you'd say he's in the process of becoming a frog. And so with you and us. We're on our way from earthly to heavenly!

Kids progress, don't they?—they metamorphose. They're one thing when they're two years old and another when they're eight or fifteen or twenty-two.

Christian, be sure of this: Just as genes dictate that a tadpole will someday be a frog, and that a baby will grow to be an adult, so God dictates that you will someday be like Christ. You're in Christ, and His meter is running.

Until we all . . . become mature, attaining to the whole measure of the fullness of Christ. (Eph. 4:13)

Confident in Christ

$\mathcal{R}$ay and I were flying when we read this paragraph in a flight magazine. It has lived with us ever since:

> Make no little plans. They have no magic to stir men's blood. . . . Make big plans. Aim high in hope and work. . . . Let your watchword be order, and your beacon, beauty.*

Let your mind expand! Believe that God will do through you large, wonderful things—and that He'll get all the credit. Call on his Holy Spirit to tell you what to ask for. Then your requests will be much bigger and more important and exciting than if you were on your own.

Don't be the kind of person who looks at the Lord through the wrong end of a telescope. Don't see Him as small. He owns everything, and He has all power. He distributes the world's commodities of time and materiel and power to whomever He pleases. And this God asks us to ask Him for things! He says, "If you remain in me and my words remain in you, ask whatever you wish, and it will be given you" (John 15:7).

Remaining or staying close in Him, and letting His words sink deep into you—those are the magic keys.

Then here's what will happen. Just as a clay pot takes its shape from its mold, so will your will be formed in the mold of the will of God. And you will have everything your own way!

It's the old saying, "Love God, and do as you please." Because when you perfectly love Him, *you will please what He pleases*.

Joanna: A Story of Renewal

---

*Daniel H. Burnham, architect on the Chicago City Plan, quoted in *Air California*, May 1980.

Here's a remarkable thing: the Bible not only describes Jesus, it describes you. His likeness is there—but so is yours. God gives you in His Word a picture of what He means for you to be:

> "Completely humble and gentle, . . . patient" (Eph. 4:2)
>
> "Strong in the Lord and in his mighty power" (Eph. 6:10)
>
> "Without complaining or arguing" (Phil. 2:14)
>
> "Not anxious," guarded by peace (Phil. 4:6–7)
>
> Forgiving, loving (Col. 3:13–14)
>
> Encouraging one another (1 Thess. 5:11)
>
> Respectful of leadership (1 Thess. 5:12)
>
> Always joyful (1 Thess. 5:16)
>
> Continually praying (1 Thess. 5:17)
>
> Giving thanks in all circumstances (1 Thess. 5:18)
>
> Avoiding every kind of evil (1 Thess. 5:22)
>
> Hard working (2 Thess. 3:11–13)
>
> Watching for the Lord's return (1 Thess. 1:10)
>
> "More than conquerors" (Rom. 8:37)!

So *love the Scriptures*. Search there for God's picture of your own intended image and likeness, and then seek to fulfill through your own life and personality exactly what you see. Make it your aim!

The result? You will—

> "reflect the Lord's glory, [and be] transformed into his [own] likeness with ever-increasing glory, which comes from the Lord" (2 Cor. 3:18)!

Fix Your Eyes on Jesus

I have a dream," said Martin Luther King. Everyone has to have a dream, to get anyplace.

A dream is a precious, exciting thing that carries you forward from day to day; a goal down the way that keeps you on the straight road to get there, looking neither to the right nor to the left; a purpose just for you alone, exhilarating enough to give you momentum for a long time to come.

Jesus came with the life goal "to seek and to save that which was lost" (Luke 19:10 KJV). This gave great pressure and urgency to his decision-making. At one point he even said, "I must journey on today and tomorrow and the next day; for it cannot be that a prophet should perish outside of Jerusalem!" (Luke 13:33 NASB).

The apostle Paul knew where he was going; he wrote, "Therefore I run in such a way, as not without aim" (1 Cor. 9:26 NASB).

Similarly, Solomon wrote,

> Let your eyes look directly ahead,
> And let your gaze be fixed straight in front of
>   you.
> Watch the path of your feet,
> And all your ways will be established.
> Do not turn to the right nor to the left;
> Turn your foot from evil.
>   (*Prov. 4:25–27* NASB)

Disciplines of the Beautiful Woman

*W*hat are your papers, your magazines, your books? They tell volumes about whether you're a dawdler, like a sheep nibbling on any tuft of grass that comes along, or whether you're going after what's important to you. They represent a quiet part of your life—part of your ship's keel. They should be a reflection of the depths of you.

You have a special interest; what is it? Housekeeping? Ham radio? Dog training? High-diving? Collect books on whatever turns you on; subscribe to a magazine on the subject; find a pen pal with the same interest; clip and file articles. Get to really know what you know!

Eliminate and concentrate! Throw the rest of the clutter away; better yet, recycle the paper stuff and give the old unread books to a library or the Salvation Army. But begin to build a personal library which is truly meaningful to you.

Most important, every Christian needs to become a specialist in God!

Many of your magazines, books, and papers need to feed your spirit. These lives of ours are to get us ready for eternity, you know! So we must "be diligent [or study, as the King James Version says] to present [ourselves] approved to God as [workmen] who [do] not need to be ashamed, handling accurately the word of truth" (2 Tim. 2:15 NASB). We need to be knowledgeable women—knowledgeable in doctrine and in Christian world affairs. This world globe has a timetable with it; we need to be alert, discerning the times and living with care.

Submerge as much of your day as you can to make it your invisible keel, by eliminating less important things. You need time to look into the face of God, time to read and study his Word systematically, time to think and plan for your life, time to praise, time to intercede, time to get wisdom for handling people and for making decisions.

Disciplines of the Beautiful Woman

The more you believe in your future, keep your eyes on it, and move toward it, the more strongly it will influence and shape you.

Start training your mind to look up and look beyond, to see God and to see your future, to get both faith and hope.

Get tough! Endure! Eyes forward!

> Forgetting those things which are behind [wrote the apostle Paul] and reaching forward to those things which are ahead, I press toward the goal for the prize of the upward call of God in Christ Jesus. (Phil. 3:13–14 NKJV)

In the midst of struggle, when you remember what's coming, you feel hope. Hope lifts and exhilarates. It expands your lungs and redoubles your energies. The hassles of the present seem easier.

Wasn't it a stroke of genius on the part of God to set us up a tremendous future and let us know it's coming?

Says Romans 8:18–19 (NKJV),

> The sufferings of this present time are not worthy to be compared with the glory which shall be revealed in us. For the earnest expectation of the creation eagerly waits for the revealing of the sons of God.

If you're reminiscing too much, you're dying.

Eyes ahead. Forward march. Is there a river before you? Wade in. The cold current will galvanize your bones. A mountain beyond the far bank? Move on. Move up . . . up . . . up. . . . *

You Don't Have to Quit

---

*James Hefley, *Life Changes*.

$\mathcal{E}$verybody's asking the question, "Who am I? Can't I discover my true identity? Don't I have the right to know?" Thomas Howard recently wrote that neither dogs nor even angels seem to be puzzled by the fact *that* they are, let alone *who* they are. Only recent humans seem to be all engrossed in the Big Question.

But Mr. Howard asks, "What is it that God seems to spend his time trying to get across to us in his Word?

> What does [God] say? Thou shalt love the Lord thy God. . . . Follow me. Be kind. . . . Be faithful. . . .
>
> "Yes, [you say] yes of course. All that. But is there a word about my self image? Can you tell me how to come to terms with myself? After all, I must find out who I am before I can do anything else."
>
> Must you? *To him that overcometh will I give a white stone, and in the stone a new name written, which no man knoweth saving he that receiveth it.* Your identity, perhaps, is a great treasure, precious beyond your wildest imaginings, kept for you by that great Custodian of souls, to be given you at the Last Day when all things are made whole. [Intriguing? He goes on to say,] This acute self-consciousness and self-scrutiny that has been laid on us by the sciences of the last hundred years may be a burden beyond our capacity to manage. Our ids may be there, so to speak, but they are none of our business, just as the fruit in Eden was there but was not healthy for us to chew on.*

"Health" is that state of affairs in which our insides are working quietly and efficiently so we can get on with the job.

Joanna: A Story of Renewal

---

*Thomas Howard, "Who Am I? Who Am I?" *Christianity Today*, 8 July 1977.

*P*aul had in mind only *one thing:*

> One thing I do: Forgetting what is behind and straining toward what is ahead, I press on toward the goal to win the prize for which God has called me heavenward in Christ Jesus. (Phil. 3:13–14)

"Forgetting what is behind"! We're little amateur psychologists these days, trying to remember all our pasts—bringing up why our mothers did this and our fathers did that—to explain all our idiosyncrasies and quirks.

The Bible doesn't so deal with us. It pronounces us sinners and then says to *get on with it,* to look up and forward! All the great people of faith in Hebrews 11 *looked forward.* So did Jesus: He endured the cross "for the joy set before him" (Heb. 12:2).

Then, with Paul, we must strain toward what's ahead and fix our attention on that: all God's promises, all our inheritance, and the goal, the prize—Jesus Himself!

"One thing I do," says Paul. It's "one-thing" believers who shed the clutter and baggage and *get there.* They "eliminate and concentrate," and they *make it.*

Take David, for instance:

> *One thing* I ask of the LORD, this is what I seek: that I may dwell in the house of the LORD all the days of my life, to gaze upon the beauty of the LORD and to seek him in his temple. (Ps. 27:4, italics mine)

Or take Mary. She sat at the feet of Jesus. And he said to her bustling sister Martha, "Only *one thing* is needed. Mary has chosen what is better, and it will not be taken away from her" (Luke 10:42, italics mine).

Be a "one-thing" Christian! Focus! Concentrate! Press on—and up!

Women's Devotional Bible

207

On what are you focusing, as a woman? What will God have you be and do?

He will not say at the judgment, "I excuse you from this or that because your husband didn't cooperate," or "I understand that you didn't have time to know My Word because of your job. . . ." No one, nothing, must keep you from putting God first in your life. You would have all eternity to be sorry.

We must all know intellectually and experientially that God is first. He must be our lives—in a class all by Himself. Everything in our lives must converge at that one point: Christ. That's the only way we'll become integrated, focused, whole women. Jesus said, "Any kingdom divided against itself is laid waste; and any city or house divided against itself shall not stand" (Matt. 12:25 NASB). Are you divided against yourself?

I've been learning that functioning as a pastor's wife, as Ray's wife, or speaking, teaching, composing, writing, mothering—none of the good things in my life dare be a substitute for the best. God can have no competition in your heart, or in mine.

Are you saying, "I'm really afraid of total surrender; I've got so many dreams and plans, and I'm not sure what would happen to them if I give myself totally to God"?

The first Queen Elizabeth asked a man to go abroad for her on business.

"I sincerely wish I could, but I can't," said the man. "My business is very demanding. It would really suffer if I left."

"Sir," replied the Queen, "if you will attend to my business, I will take care of your business."

Work out the implications in your own life of putting God first.

Disciplines of the Beautiful Woman

*A*bide in Christ! *Stay in Him! Live His plan for you with all your might! Be happy in Him; be happy in your life in Him; be happy in all He gives you and in all He takes away; be happy in what you do; be happy in what you can't do; be happy in all He makes you to be; be happy in what He never allows you to be. Be happy in you! Be happy in Him!*

No more drifting, wandering, doubting, complaining, living in confusion.

Don't let anyone judge you (Col. 2:16).

Don't let anyone disqualify you (Col. 2:18).

Don't let anyone discourage you (2 Chron. 20:15).

Don't let anyone deter you (Mark 9:39a).

Don't let anyone detract you from your goal (James 1:4).

God has made you alive with Christ (Col. 2:13), and you have been given fullness in Him (Col. 2:10). He is a shield around you, your Glorious One, Who lifts up your head (Ps. 3:3).

Then, from your stance in Christ, produce! Achieve! GOFORIT!

Perhaps you'll become so focused, so concentrated, that your sunbeam will narrow to a laser beam. People like this become the geniuses, the prophets, the ones with maximum intensity of power to affect.

Open yourself wide to whatever He desires.

Disciplines of the Heart

*O*n what few things can you put your faith without wavering? Let's look at ultimates, at what will last forever, as predicted by the only final authority, God.

1. *You can put your faith in the Church. It has ultimate staying power.* Jesus prophesied that the gates of hell would not overcome it (see Matt. 16:18). The Spirit predicted "glory in the church . . . throughout all generations, for ever and ever! Amen" (Eph. 3:21).

Don't be too bugged by the worldwide church's temporary sidetracks and divisions and foolishnesses. Whatever they are, let your love for the Church have staying power. God's does.

2. *You can put your faith in the Bible. It, too, has ultimate staying power.* Every generation hears a reincarnation of the serpent's words in the Garden, some new twist of doctrine which questions, "Did God really say . . . ?" (see Gen. 3:1).

Settle it once and for all, that you will trust the Bible.

> Your word, O LORD is eternal;
>   it stands firm in the heavens. (Ps. 119:89)

3. *You can also put your faith in your coming future, God's future inheritance for you.* What is it we believers are going to get, later on? Nobody knows. It's a surprise. But we know it will be wonderful, and we know it, also, will have ultimate staying power.

> In his great mercy [God] has given us new birth into a living
> hope . . . and into an inheritance that can never perish,
> spoil or fade—kept in heaven for you. (1 Pet. 1:3–4)

4. *You can put your trust in the Source of all staying power, God Himself.*

You Don't Have to Quit

Now we ask you, brothers, to respect those who work
hard among you, who are over you in the Lord and who ad-
monish you. Hold them in the highest regard in love because
of their work. Live in peace with each other. And we urge
you, brothers, warn those who are idle, encourage the timid,
help the weak, be patient with everyone. Make sure that
nobody pays back wrong for wrong, but always try to be kind
to each other and to everyone else. (1 Thess. 5:12–15)

*O*h, all of us who are children of God! How untaught we
are in how to treat each other! How distracted we are by our
lonely pursuits! How numb we are to each other's private pain!
How totally desperate some of us are to know and to be
known—to have someone, or just a few, who really care!

What do strangers look for in a new church? They want one
that's "friendly." So the pastor tries to get his people to smile
and shake hands with visitors, but it's not easy. They hardly do
it to each other; why should they with someone they don't
know? And so most Christianity turns out seeming so anesthe-
tized, so cold, so drugged—as if it's about to sink down into the
snows of death.

This book is a shout, a scream, a call: Fuse, brothers, fuse!
Put away whatever is dividing you! Sign a pact with your blood!
Place yourselves deeply, deeply together—whatever its awk-
wardness or pain!

Reach anew to God, then reach to each other. Only then
can you reach out to the world.

Discipling One Another

Be devoted to one another in brotherly love. (Rom. 12:10)

*T*he hunger for meaningful Christian togetherness has grown enormous in today's world. And I think the hunger is intensified by the fact of our actual shyness, our inhibitions, our clumsiness in handling each other.

Think about your average married partners. In their minds are wild, wonderful dreams of how they'd like to treat each other, sizzling straight off the pages of novels! But in reality? They'd be terrified of anything a cut above tepid and predictable.

Don't you think most of us Christians are the same? We love to talk and dream "relationships," but in actuality our own often seem to be self-serving, phoney, disappointing, or at least just unappealing.

We need to look hard at the Bible's kind of love.

It's realistic.

It's tender.

It's aggressive.

It's tenacious.

It's jealous.

It's forever.

It's emotional.

It's total.

It's unspeakably sweet.

It's tough!

God loves us with tough love . . . and that's the way we need to learn to love each other.

Discipling One Another

*A*cts 2:4 says that all the believers were filled with the Holy Spirit. That is totally unifying. There is nothing exclusive or discriminatory about it.

When we share the Spirit of Christ and concentrate on him, differences shrink down, or melt away. If we settle into secondary things, we'll bicker and argue: if we're occupied, for instance, with details of the regulations we set for our lifestyles; or with liturgies, ceremonies, and church customs; or with secondary doctrinal issues; or with affairs of government, political parties, national issues, and so on.

We're drawn and held together by the Spirit on the basics: God, sin, death, sacrifice, love. We must stay solidly on the basics to maintain unity and sweetness.

Recently Ray and Nels and I sat on some grass and listened to a beautiful symphony orchestra. Hundreds of us, probably greatly diverse in our lives and philosophies, were unified as we were caught up into the same beauty!

Christian, minimize in your thinking the differences between you and other believers! Seek to be caught up together in the beauty of Jesus Christ, and be "lost in wonder, love, and praise."

Discipling One Another

Make every effort to keep the unity of the Spirit through the bond of peace. There is one body and one spirit—just as you were called to one hope when you were called—one Lord, one faith, one baptism, one God and Father of all, who is over all and through all and in all. (Eph. 4:3–4)

*H*ave you ever been sad over the split of those former partners, Barnabas and Paul, in Acts 15:39–40? You remember the story. Paul and Barnabas were traveling and preaching, and picked up Barnabas's cousin John Mark (Col. 4:10) to go along with them. Later when the going got rough, Mark deserted. Barnabas could forgive him and later wanted to sign him up again, but Paul said "nothing doing." And the debate got so hot that Barnabas took Mark and went off to preach, and Paul took a new partner, Silas (Acts 15:36–41).

Barnabas had been wonderful from Acts 4:36 on. What happened that he lost his head? After the fight we never hear of him again, unless it's that sad little note about him in Galatians 2:13.

The issue wasn't doctrine but personality. The issue wasn't who was right. I suppose, actually, Paul was the rigid one—he was so dedicated, he couldn't stand for Barnabas's relative Mark to be less dedicated. Our little saying, "If Christ is not Lord of all, he is not Lord at all," can make us too tough and unforgiving and critical, can't it! (Acknowledging Christ's "lordship" is a growing thing.)

It's not easy to be a member of the family of God. You can't have close relationships without occasionally getting hurt, just the way you do in a physical family. But be careful not to get to be a fussy, divisive, critical Christian!

Even our profound convictions are not infallible. Let's leave room for others' convictions, even though we remain true to our own. Unity is so precious, it must be highly prized, sought after, and maintained!

Discipling One Another

*T*he loving church has a wonderful fragrance about it. Love each other—period!—not because of worth!

Gilbert Tennant was a Presbyterian pastor in Philadelphia in 1750, during the days of the Great Awakening. In a Lake Avenue Church sermon, Ray describes one of Tennant's sermons like this:

> He urged his congregation to love each other, and love each other to the end. He said when you begin to love each other you come to a certain place—oh, hear me, my friends!—you come at a certain place when you discover the real truth.
>
> And in every one of our lives there's a can of worms. Believe you me! There's a skeleton in the closet of every life here. And you see, we can be willing to be known, or we can be willing to know, up to that point. That's it.
>
> That's safe, but that's superficial. But, [Tennant] says, you must love right in through that painful area . . . love right on to the end. Refuse to let go, though you know everything about that person. Refuse to let go! . . .
>
> Fragile love will love up to a point, and that's not worth anything. That's what most Christians experience. But there are those who are willing to know and willing to be known to the point where they go crashing right on through that threshold of pain—to where they really know and are known!

There's a bumper sticker I see sometimes on the backs of cars that says, "Christians aren't perfect; they're just forgiven."

Discipling One Another

> People who want to get rich fall into temptation and a trap
> and into many foolish and harmful desires that plunge men
> into ruin and destruction. (1 Tim. 6:9)

*S*ounds as if we have to choose between money and God.
Not at all!

It's like dog training. When food arrives on the scene, a
bad-mannered dog will lunge and tear at it and grab all he can
get. With training he learns to control himself and wait pa-
tiently until his master gives it to him—and gives him the
amount that the dog's best health requires.

A Christian who doesn't trust God to feed him will grab for
all he can get—not understanding that God says that "godliness
with contentment is *great gain*" (1 Tim. 6:6, emphasis added)!
God will feed you well if you let Him feed you on His terms,
while you give yourself to worthier concerns.

You've seen what we've seen: people so wild for money that
they shipwreck themselves on the rocks of tension, adultery,
overdrinking, instability, fights, bankruptcies, and, in general,
"the crazies." Their little ones pay a terrible price, and so do
they.

> For the love of money is a root of all kinds of evil. Some
> people, eager for money, have wandered from the faith and
> pierced themselves with many griefs. (1 Tim. 6:10)

> *You Don't Have to Quit*

216

*W*e've got to learn to "hang looser" about possessions in the family of God. There were lots of Old Testament laws even to legislate this kind of attitude:

You weren't to charge interest on a loan to a fellow Israelite, only to a foreigner. (That meant one who didn't know God—[Deut. 23:19–20].)

If you requested payment on a loan, you were to stand outside a fellow Israelite's house, not go in. Then you wouldn't seem too pushy (Deut. 24:10–11).

When you harvested your crops, you weren't to pick clean. You were to leave some fruit on the tree, or leave your fallen wheat on the ground, for the needy and the stranger (Lev. 19:9–10).

You were to pay salaries immediately, and pay any debts as soon as you had the money. You weren't to hold it when you had it (Deut. 24:15).

You could always eat freely from any neighbor's property what you could carry in your hand. You just couldn't bring your baskets! (Deut. 23:24).

And so on. There was a strong sense of ownership and pride of ownership and respect for ownership. But at the same time, the edges were to slop over and nobody was to get uptight about it. They were to learn to be generous and loose with each other—because God is that way with all of us!

Discipling One Another

Keep your lives free from the love of money and be content with what you have, because God has said, "Never will I leave you; never will I forsake you." (Heb. 13:5)

Do good, . . . be rich in good deeds, . . . be generous and willing to share. (1 Tim. 6:18)

Our friend Jim says, "Boy, it was so freeing when I discovered that my income isn't my source of supply, God is! God knows my needs; my income doesn't know my needs! So I don't depend on my income, I depend on Him."

> The eyes of all look to you,
>> and you give them their food at the proper
>>> time.
> You open your hand
>> and satisfy the desires of every living thing.
>>> (Ps. 145:15–16)

To be dependent on your own supplies is bondage. To be dependent on Him (the One who promises over and over to supply your need)—*this is freedom.*

You can't support yourself any more than you could create yourself. Leave to God the things that only God can do.

So don't fix your eyes on your bills, your problems, your needs—He "knows that you need them" (Matt. 6:32).

Fix your eyes on Jesus.

Fix Your Eyes on Jesus

If . . . God clothes the grass of the field, which is here today and tomorrow is thrown into the fire, will he not much more clothe you, O you of little faith? So do not worry. . . . The pagans run after all these things. (Matt. 6:30–32)

𝒫astor John was continuing his series of sermons on renewal, and today he was reaching from Mark 14:3: "While [Jesus] was in Bethany, reclining at a table in the home of a man known as Simon the Leper, a woman [John identifies her as Jesus' friend, Mary] came with an alabaster jar of very expensive perfume, made of pure nard. She broke the jar and poured the perfume on his head."

"Mary poured out a very expensive gift," said the pastor. "And that's what worship is.

"We worship as we give back to Him of that which He has given us—and it must be in some way proportionate to His giving, or it's just plain silly.

"God says to us, 'I love you,' and with that He 'graciously gives us all things'—Romans 8:32. If we say, 'I love you, too, Lord' and offer him a dollar bill, He must say, 'You gotta be kidding . . .'

"Mary gave so much that everyone around her was shocked. But Jesus didn't say, 'Now, Mary, I understand your heart, but you take back half of this. After all, you've got your expenses. God helps those who help themselves. He wants you to use your common sense, too.'

"No, He said, 'I tell you the truth, wherever the gospel is preached throughout the world, what she has done will also be told, in memory of her'—verse 9. And twenty centuries later, I'm here still fulfilling that prediction.

"Ladies and gentlemen," said Pastor John earnestly, as he leaned over the pulpit, "are you really learning what it means to worship God? Oh, how I long for you to! Are you learning what it really means to tell Him you love Him?

"His love was sacrificial; yours must be, too. Any love that is not costly is phoney."

Joanna: A Story of Renewal

219

*N*ow about collections," wrote Paul. "You Corinthians do the same thing I told the Galatians to do." (In other words, it's a good general plan.) "Set aside a sum of money in proportion with your income on each first day of the week" (see 1 Cor. 16:2).

(You Seventh-Day Adventists and Messianic Jews may bring it on the seventh day, but it's still weekly.)

Oh, what a thrill! What a great idea! God says to lay aside a gift to Him *weekly*. He knows very well that many of us get paid less often than that. Ray's salary comes bimonthly. We divide the Lord's amount into four equal checks—which means that when five-Sunday months come along, not of our planning, they allow us the scary thrill of giving twenty-five percent more. Remember, we don't give at our convenience; we give weekly what we've decided in our heart ahead of time to give (2 Cor. 9:7).

Here's how we do it. When the paycheck arrives we write all God's checks first, put them in predated envelopes, and place them on our dresser. Every time we see them we can pray over them and anticipate the thrill of giving. Sunday morning the envelope goes into my Bible, sticking out of the pages. I've trained myself to walk in the church doors saying in my heart, "Father, I come to You bringing our offering. We love You. It's our sacrifice to tell You so."

How much do you give? Don't say, "Well, never enough!" Then you're training yourself to expect to under-give. *You can give enough.* God will show you what's the right amount in proportion to your income, and you'll have the wonderful joy of obedience in giving! *It will be big,* for you. Leave the "tipping" to unbelievers, who don't understand.

But you'll always have enough for the rest of living. Always. Second Corinthians 9:6–8.

Up with Worship

*H*ere's an old-fashioned illustration that's so good I can't think of a more modern one to replace it.*A piece of iron, in itself and by itself, is cold, black, hard, and ugly. But hold it in a furnace, and what a change takes place!

I saw that once with my own eyes at Lukens Steel Mill in Coatesville, Pennsylvania. The coldness was gone, the blackness was gone, the hardness was gone, the ugliness was gone— the iron had been transformed. The fire and the iron were still distinguishable from each other; the iron was certainly still iron. But as long as that iron was held in the fire, it had entered into a new experience, and it was hot and glowing and purified.

You ask me what I, Anne Ortlund, am in myself, and I can tell you that I'm "cold, black, hard, and ugly"! But as long as I remain in the fire of Christ, I'm hot and glowing and purified. From moment to moment it's my privilege to remain there, to "abide in Him"—and He Himself is my life and purity and power. Only He sets me free from the law of sin and death (Rom. 8:2)—but, oh, He does set me free!

Can I boast that this is true? Hey, I know very well what I am in myself.

Do I "know the Lord"? I've barely begun. Just the same, as Meister Eckhart said, "No one knows better what heat is than the man who is hot.†

Abide in me, and [I will] abide in you. (John 15:4)

Come near to God and he will come near to you. (James 4:8)

Disciplines of the Heart

---

*Illustration taken from *The Message of Keswick*.

† *Meister Eckhart*, ed. James M. Clark.

$\mathcal{W}$e need to see how cold, black, hard, and ugly we are, to get motivated to stay in that fire. Unless we do, we will never hate sin and fear sin and be repelled by sin enough to stay in the fire. (Says Tozer, "The Holy Spirit is first of all a moral flame.")

We *are* deteriorating morally. With so many out of the fire, we're cooling off and getting black. I see evangelical Christianity passing from the wonderful height of its acceptance *IN* this world to the depth of its acceptance *OF* this world.

I see how, when liberalism waned and we evangelicals rose to popularity and were listened to, we could have given our authentic message and cried to the world, "Repent! Be radically cleansed of your sin! Receive Jesus Christ's purity and holiness for your lives!"

But instead, in that time of golden opportunity, we lost our courage. We became embarrassed by our "separation" from the world, and we cozied up to it and joined it. We Madison-Avenue-trivialized our glorious gospel. And we stained ourselves with the world's adulteries and fornications.

We must weep; we must mourn! We must hate what He hates! Let us ask Him to forgive our unwashed praises before Him, our sillinesses, our ignorances.

Let us see how our coldness, blackness, hardness, ugliness become colder, blacker, harder, uglier—unless in terror we wrench ourselves free and rush to His precious Fire!

> *God our Father,*
> *Lord Jesus Christ our Saviour,*
> *Holy Spirit, purifying, white-hot Fire,*
>   *We rush to You.*

Disciplines of the Heart

Let me describe what Pentecost *wasn't* like, all right?

Picture all those believers meeting together; suddenly there's fire on their heads!! And there's the sound of a mighty, rushing wind, and it fills all the house where they're sitting.

"Great! This is wonderful!" they cry. "Quick! Shut the windows! Let's capture this glorious wind forever!"

So twenty, thirty years later, there they sit—faces flushed, eyes glazed, remembering the day God came—and determined to keep everything exactly as it was then.

My friend, the wind is a *wind*. You can't trap it, you just have to go with it. Thus it is with the Holy Spirit!

Past successes can completely undo you, Christian, and undo your church, too. God blessed something wonderfully awhile back; it was so beautiful; so you work at it, you fan it, you wear out the saints trying to revive it. But, friend, God has gone on to something else—and you don't even know it!

Forget yesterday; today is God's precious gift. His name is "I AM." He is forever contemporary.

Christians who stay with Him are the same—they're happy, "now" people.

Churches who stay with Him are happy, "now" churches. "The old has gone, the new has come!" (2 Cor. 5:17). "Forgetting the past, they press on to what lies ahead" (Phil. 3:13, paraphrase).

They are characterized by wind and fire; they blow clean, they burn clean.

Up with Worship

223

*A*bram and Sarai were married before their story ever begins in Genesis 11. You just can't imagine them apart.

. . . Years pass. Then together they're rewarded with changed names. The Lord God Almighty appears and says to Abram, "No longer will you be called Abram [Exalted Father]; your name will be Abraham [Father of Multitudes]!" (Gen. 17:5).

What's the difference? Just one sound: the letter "H"—the sound of breath. God breathes into Abram's name: "Your name will be Abrah-h-h-ham."

A marvel! God had long ago breathed into Adam, and he became a living person (Gen. 2:7). Years later Jesus would breathe His Holy Spirit into His disciples (John 20:22). (Both the Hebrew and Greek words for "breath" and "spirit" are the same.)

God breathes into Sarai's name as well. He says to Abraham, "You are no longer to call her Sarai; her name will be Sarah-h-h-h."

An exquisite reward, a spiritual high point, a new beginning in their lives.

From then on, when people (even God?) pronounced the names "Abraham" and "Sarah," they used extra breath. And God's Holy Spirit was a new breathing upon them, a new empowering from heaven.

Does your "name," that is, your reputation, have about it the impression that God is breathing into it? "The wind blows wherever it pleases. . . . So it is with everyone born of the Spirit" (John 3:8). Do others think of you as flexible, fresh, blown along by the Holy Spirit (see 2 Pet. 1:21)? This will be true if you are filled with Him.

And that's His command to you in Ephesians 5:18. Then ask the Holy Spirit right now to breathe into you His fullness.

Disciplines of the Home

$\mathcal{A}$ mother once took her little boy to hear Paderewski, the great pianist. At the beginning there was simply a bare stage with a spotlight focused on the grand piano and bench. The mother and son had come half an hour early, and eventually the little boy got restless. Somehow, the mother got absorbed in reading the program, and when she finally looked up, his seat was empty! She looked everywhere around her, and he was no-where to be seen.

Then—her heart was in her throat—suddenly she heard the sound of "Chopsticks." There he was on stage, in the spot-light, picking away on the long concert grand!

"Get him out of there!" came voices from the crowd.

"No!" cried a European accent from the wings, and the great Paderewski strode on stage. "Boy, keep going. I'll help you."

And he sat down on the bench next to the little fellow and began adding fabulous improvisations—chords, patterns, runs, and additional melodies—as the two of them entranced the packed house with "Variations on Chopsticks"!

> In the same way, the Spirit helps us in our weakness. We do not know what we ought to pray for, but the Spirit himself intercedes for us with groans that words cannot express. And he who searches our hearts knows the mind of the Spirit, because the Spirit intercedes for the saints in accordance with God's will." (Rom. 8:26–27)

When we pick at our pathetic little prayers—when we live our pathetic little lives—suddenly we are not alone. Someone has come alongside us—none other than the Almighty Spirit of God!—and we have moved into a duet of greatness beyond our dreams.

Joanna: A Story of Renewal

*A*nne: "Joanna."

Joanna: "Yes?"

Anne: "I'd like to introduce myself. I'm Anne Ortlund."

Joanna: "I don't believe I know that name."

Anne: "Well, I write, and I plan for you to be the lead character in this book. (I'm not asking you; I'm telling you!)"

Joanna: "Really? . . . It could be fun.

"But how will you describe me? Will you play me up right? I mean, the idea makes me a little nervous when I don't know what you'd say. After all, I'm doing pretty well, and I'd like people to know it. Will you write that David is very successful, that we live in an oceanview home in Newport Beach, and that we have two fantastic kids in the best colleges? Will you describe my looks and what I wear?"

Anne: "Joanna, I'll say all that, but this is a book to picture how a person gets spiritually renewed. I'd like to bring you from your present self as a complacent, nominal Christian to what you can be—an alive and growing Christian in touch with God in thrilling reality."

Joanna: "Look, I'm not sure I want you tinkering with me. I'm doing all right! David and I go to church; we've got great friends; and we live decent, good lives. But I'm not the emotional type. I steer clear of all that fanatic, halleluia stuff."

Anne: "Joanna, your greatest need is something that's unfamiliar to you, so you're avoiding it.

"Like many of the potential readers of this book, your Christian life is stagnated and you hardly know it. Your spiritual sensitivity has gotten dulled—and you're almost unaware of it.

"But now and then you wonder if your life could be different . . . and better. Isn't that true?"

Joanna: A Story of Renewal

T read Ecclesiastes 12:12–13 with both a chuckle and a twinge of fear:

> Be warned, my son. . . . Of making many books there is no end,
>   and much study wearies the body.
>   Now all has been heard;
>   here is the conclusion of the matter:
>   Fear God and keep his commandments,
>   for this is the whole duty of man.

I must not be writing-centered; you must not be reading-centered. We must both be God-centered! Back to God Himself! Back to "priority one"!

"The conclusion is . . . : fear God."

He is the Source,
      the Center,
      the Fullness,
      the Target,
      the Completion,
      of everything, everywhere . . .
      of the universe . . .
      of your heart in this moment.

As you're reading, tell Him "Alleluia."

Disciplining One Another

*D*avid," said Joanna, "there's a lot I don't understand yet. But the greatest commandment is, 'Love the Lord your God with all your heart, and with all your soul, and with all your strength.'" (Even as she verbalized God's Word, she felt Him renewing her and putting words in her mouth.)

"This is the God of my childhood. *He* isn't new, but *I'm* getting new. I'm just discovering that the reason my life has been so dull and unproductive and meaningless is that I've made no attempt to love Him in the way He asks me to."

They were not far away from where the little Fiat was parked, and Joanna retrieved her notebook.

"Listen, David," she said, "I can't say it well on my own. Let me read you some of my notes:

> "God told Abraham in Genesis 12:1, 'Leave your country; get away from your father's house. . . .'
>
> "God was saying to Abraham, 'Leave your old habits, your routines, your lifestyle—all that determines your life and holds you prisoner, all that which seems normal only because it's so familiar to you, and everyone else does it.
>
> "'Come to Me!' He says. 'Start fresh! Shuck off the unworthy. Let Me rearrange you, put you together.'
>
> "This takes time. Put yourself under Him a good while every day. Sit at His feet. Let Him teach you, correct you, do what He wants to do with you."

"I'm starting to do that, David," she said earnestly.

Joanna: A Story of Renewal

Do not conform any longer to the pattern of this world, but be transformed by the renewing of your mind. (Rom. 12:2)

$\mathcal{M}$y friend Reudun has white-hot spiritual fire in her bones. I love her. She accepted Christ as a teenager in her native Norway, when revival was sweeping the land. She loves to describe how people talked about Jesus continually on the streets, in the markets, in homes; how they were continually fellowshiping with each other; how it was hard to break up the church meetings because nobody wanted to quit.

"Tell me, Reudun," I asked, "did everybody in Norway become Christian in those days? Was it just sort of a blanket thing?"

"Oh, no!" she said. "Some people hardly knew it was happening. Most of the big state cathedrals went right on with their dry, empty services with a dozen little old ladies and hundreds of empty pews."

I thought of how a gusher of rain can make water pour down the side of a mountain; and if it should strike a big rock, it will just divide and go around it. And the rock will just sit there, as unmoved as though nothing were happening.

Christian, there's new life all around the world. There's excitement about Jesus; there's hunger to get back to the original Christian lifestyle; it's a new day!

Don't be one of those rocks. Don't let God's revival pass you by!

Discipling One Another

Never be lacking in zeal, but keep your spiritual fervor, serving the Lord. (Rom. 12:11)

*T*he past two thousand years have been like Israel's winter time following the early rains. There have been occasional "falls" of the Holy Spirit's blessing here and there. But the Bible predicts a latter rain of revival which will really be some "gusher," compared to the revival connected with Jesus' first coming.

That one affected only one city, Jerusalem; this will affect the whole world (Matt. 24:14).

That affected a few thousand people; this will affect unnumbered multitudes (Isa. 45:22–23).

That was an authentic rain, for sure—a spiritual "early rain," but small compared with the spring rain that will come.

D. M. Patton wrote,

> Vastly more was wrapped up in the descent of the Holy Spirit than the church has yet experienced, or than the world has yet seen; and the Spirit himself thus reveals that while the Christian centuries are "the last days," and Pentecost began the wonder, we today, standing in the last of the last, are on the edge of a second and more tremendous upheaval of the Holy Spirit.*

Discipling One Another

Will you not revive us again,
    that your people may rejoice in you?
                    (Ps. 85:6)

O Holy Ghost, revival comes from thee;
Send a revival—start the work in me.
                    —*J. Edwin Orr*

---

*Quoted by Arthur Wallis in *In The Day of Thy Power*.

*W*hen our family lived in England a few years ago we found an old church with a big front door—and over to the left, a slot in the outside wall like a letter drop. It was called the "lepers' squint"! Oh, dear God, couldn't all Your children go into church?

No, the ones with leprosy huddled around the slot in the wall and took turns peering through. *What was that last sentence? What did he say?* Bless their hearts, what a way to worship God.

Think about the whole universe—all of creation—every atom of it jammed, crammed with wisdom, morality, beauty, joy. Righteousness, space, truth, and time superimpose, synchronize, flow. How can we figure it? How can our heads get it all together?

God chooses for now to give us just a few brief clues: enough to know we must accept and love and worship Jesus Christ—plus only a few other mouth-watering glimpses into what the whole thing is about.

And all the clues, all the glimpses are in His one Book. His "lepers' squint"!

Think about it. When you open and read your Bible you're squinting through those brief, few words at God's Everything.

Listen! Listen! *What's God saying? What did He mean by that last sentence? Don't go so fast you're not getting it.*

God!

Vastness is behind Your words! Seas crashing, solar systems roaring,—and the Cross, the Cross!

Read it once more. *What was that again?*

Up with Worship

Suppose a little boy looks through the knothole of a fence to see a parade.

If he sees a clown pass by, he's tickled. If he sees a lion, he's afraid. If there's a space in between, he may think the parade's over. If someone blocks his view, he may think there's no parade at all.

But suppose a man picks him up. He puts him on his shoulders, above the line of the fence. Then he can see a good part of the parade all at once, and he gets the idea! Indeed, if he were higher *up* he might see the entire parade in one view.

"Now we see through a knothole," many of us. All we can see at one moment is that our checkbook is empty, or our husband is sick, and we get thoroughly discouraged.

Up with Worship

But God's Word is a helicopter! It shows you the whole parade—what has been, what is now in view, and what will be. Check out the breathtaking parade still to come:

> Look, [Christ] is coming with the clouds,
>   and every eye will see him,
> even those who pierced him;
>   and all the peoples of the earth shall mourn
>   because of him. (Rev. 1:7)

Dear children, continue in him, so that when he appears we may be confident and unashamed before him at his coming. (1 John 2:28)

So remember David's words,

> The law of the LORD is perfect, reviving the soul.
> The statutes of the LORD are trustworthy, making
>   wise the simple. (Ps. 19:7)

*D*r. Donald Grey Barnhouse was an American preacher of the last generation, and he had a sparkle like nobody else.

One time he was telling his audience why they needed to read the whole Bible. He reminded them how God said to Abraham, "I'm going to give you this land (Palestine), so go walk around it. Every place you set your foot will be yours" (loose wording of Gen. 13:14, 17; Deut. 11:24; and Josh. 1:3).

The way Dr. Barnhouse told it, that evening Abraham took a walk, and he walked around about an acre—and that night he owned an acre.

And the next day he walked around a mile, and he owned the mile.

And when the sheep had grazed all that space, he took them over to the next valley, and he owned the valley. ("Every place where you set your foot will be yours.")

It wasn't too many years until he owned everything from Dan to Beersheba—just by putting his foot down.

And, said Dr. Barnhouse with his sparkle, lots of Christians possess a very small Bible. They have John 3:16 and the Twenty-third Psalm and a few other little passages, and they keep going back and forth from one to another, maybe grazing those little spots down to bare rock. And that's all they have.

And God says, "Go, walk through the length and breadth of the land! Every place where you set your foot will be yours"— all of God's Word, full of wonderful truths just for you.

Take up your Bible; look at it. The land is before you, ready for you to possess.

And *Jesus is there!* "Handle me, and see," He says (Luke 24:39 KJV).

Read your Bible from cover to cover.

Fix Your Eyes on Jesus

233

Υou know the New Testament is about Christ. But the Old Testament was written centuries before; is that about Him, too? "Absolutely," said Jesus: "These are the Scriptures that testify about me" (John 5:39).

Take a look.

In the Old Testament's very first book God promised Abraham, "For all the land which thou seest, to thee will I give it, and to thy seed for ever" (Gen. 13:15 KJV).

And two thousand years later in the New Testament, the Spirit of God explains that He was talking back there about Jesus Christ: "He saith not, 'And to seeds,' as of many; but as one, 'And to thy seed,' which is Christ" (Gal. 3:16 KJV).

And Peter, preaching on Pentecost, said the Psalms talked of Jesus: "David speaketh concerning him" (Acts 2:25 KJV).

Hebrews 1:8 says Psalm 45:6–7 refers to Jesus.

And around 750 B.C. the prophet Isaiah wrote, "I saw the Lord seated on a throne, high and exalted, and the train of his robe filled the temple" (Isa. 6:1). And John reveals who he saw: the preexistent Christ! "Isaiah . . . saw Jesus' glory."

You see,
  The New is in the Old contained;
  The Old is by the New explained.

From Genesis to Revelation *Jesus is there*, and *if you want to fix your eyes on Him, you must look at His entire book.** A. W. Tozer used to say, "Nothing less than a whole Bible can make a whole Christian."†

Fix Your Eyes on Jesus

---

*If you'd like to read it through next year as I do, you can order the daily help I use: *Daily Walk*, P.O. Box 478, Mt. Morris, Illinois 61054, or phone 1-800-877-5539.

† A. W. Tozer, *Still Waters, Deep Waters*.

*R*ay's first love and greatest gift, I guess, is preaching God's Word. It's certainly his passion to study the Scriptures correctly and feed his flock a balanced diet of truth. But in all his years he's never sat under expository Bible preaching; seminary helped in many practical ways, but not in learning the Bible; and he's never been to a Bible school.

So where did he learn all he knows—everything which for seventeen years has been broadcast daily halfway around the world, and taught millions? He's learned it just the way you and I can—from digging on his own. From asking good teachers for suggestions on study books. From reading the Book itself, and its marginal notes and cross references. From tracking down word studies in concordances. From praying over it. I know this, because for many years he has let me get out of town with him one day a week and study with him. What a privilege.

And you know what? Whether you're a long-time Bible student or a novice, the Holy Spirit is your personal teacher, and He will grade the material for you! Each time you read it, He'll make it right just for your level of understanding at that time. He's wonderful!

So set aside time each day; have your notebook and pencil ready. Begin with one book or one section, probably something in the New Testament if it's new to you. Note the key thoughts, key words; how the passage fits what's before and after; what you don't understand, to ask somebody; how it can help your life that very day. Dig in!

Disciplines of the Beautiful Woman

Study to shew thyself approved unto God, a workman that needeth not to be ashamed, rightly dividing the word of truth. (2 Tim. 2:15 KJV)

235

$\mathcal{R}$ecently a minister, a dear guy with a hassled look, said to Ray and me, "I want to tell you honestly that the church scene to me these days is just one blur of potlucks and committee meetings. Frankly, it's a drag. There are plenty of times when I want out."

We answered with sympathy; we have felt that way plenty!

But the analogy we used in our answer was marriage: You start off in a romantic pink cloud—but eventually, inevitably, some morning you wake up, look across at that lump in the bed with its mouth open, and you think, "I'm married to this? Yuck!" *At that point* love becomes an act of the will, and of conscious obedience to God. "I am committed to him (or her), and that's that. I *choose* to continue to love, and love with all my being." Later the pink cloud will be there again!

Ordination, we said, was a "pink cloud" experience. Eventually, inevitably, every minister wakes up to the "yuck" feeling! And *at that point,* as for every Christian, loving the Body with all our hearts becomes a conscious act of the will, a commitment-no-matter-what.

But furthermore, we said, the Christians in Acts 2:46 had potlucks, and in Acts 15:4 they had committees—and we have to see these things through spiritual eyes. What are potlucks and committees but opportunities for people to rub off on each other—people who have Jesus Christ inside, in whom is glory, whose destination is heaven?

When they interact a mystical thing is happening. And ten years later, after all the potlucks and committees with their ingredients of love and laughter, of pain and patience, of hard times and difficulties and misunderstandings and fighting our way back again to each other—after and through all that, looks of glory begin to grow on our faces!

Discipling One Another

The church . . . is his body, the fullness of him who fills
everything in every way. (Eph. 1:22–23)

I love the church!" Ray exclaimed to me recently. I know
it's true. He loves the grandparents, the children, the middle-
agers, the young people; he loves the mystics, the pragmatists,
the theologians, the simplists, the immature and the deep, the
visionaries and the plodders, the faithful committee workers
who make it happen and the laggards who have to be cajoled.
Ray loves the church! I can't pray he'll back off; I can only pray
he'll have the body and heart to love it for a long, long time.

And as his wife, I see what the church has done for Ray—
deep things I never could have done.

I told this recently to a young wife, who didn't want her
husband to serve on one of our church committees. "Let your
husband go," I said. "Don't try to overpossess him. If you don't
sense that he's deliberately escaping from his family—which is
another matter—then (I know this sounds heretical) let him
plunge into all the church life he wants to. His heart may need
it. Encourage lots of exposure to godly people. He'll be a far better husband and father as a result!"

I told her how the multifaceted, richly diverse Body of
Christ has stretched and challenged Ray in a thousand ways I
couldn't—ever—as one human being. Sometimes when he's
come home, for all the fatigue, there's a look of splendor shining in his eyes. And when he does come home, in less time he's
a far more effective husband and father. Oh, yes! The children
and I wouldn't trade.

The miracle of the church! Who can explain it? We need
all the relationships God will give us. Each believer represents
a different facet of Jesus Christ.

Discipling One Another

237

When Jesus promised Peter a hundred times as many mothers, fathers, brothers, sisters, sons, and daughters as he had ever given up, he was looking toward a rich new family that would satisfy Peter's needs better than his "household" family ever could. (And remember the *substitution* lasted only roughly a year and a half. Mostly, the spiritual family was in *addition to* —a double blessing.)

Think about it. Because of the support and input of his physical family, Peter had grown to be a mature professional fisherman with undoubtedly a sense of responsibility and many other fine qualities. Praise God for His provision of physical families, with all the nurture and support and stimulus they provide! They are the springboard for great attainment in this world.

But think of the input of Jesus and the other disciples for three years on Peter, and then the thrill of representing the Twelve in preaching on the day of Pentecost (Acts 2:14). Think of the stimulus Cornelius provided, showing Peter that the whole Gentile world was waiting to be opened up for the gospel (Acts 10). What about when he got thrown into prison and all the brothers and sisters had an all-night prayer meeting for him (Acts 12)? How about the "tough love" Paul showed Peter when he rebuked him to his face one time when he turned hypocrite (Gal. 2:11–14)? Or the awesome thrill of being considered at last one of the three pillars of the mother church in Jerusalem (Gal. 2:9)?

Over the years Peter was so intellectually and spiritually and emotionally stimulated and motivated by spiritual brothers, sisters, parents, and children, that this fisherman from up-country Galilee wrote two of our greatest pieces of literature.

Discipling One Another

To the elders among you, I appeal as a fellow elder . . . be shepherds of God's flock. (1 Pet. 5:1–2)

*I*n these days the church may seem to us a ragtag affair without much rhyme or reason. That's because we're looking at the tapestry on the wrong side, with all its yarn ends showing. Just wait till eternity and we'll see the church on the other side, where God sees it! Oh, glory! Dazzling brilliance and splendor!

Don't bad-mouth the church, Christian. Don't put any activity or group, not even any parachurch movement, above the church. The church is Christ's Body.

Now, I understand that there's a difference between the visible church and the invisible. I know that the local "First Church" on the corner downtown is probably a mixture of true believers and fakes. But precisely because we don't have the eyes to see which is which, we'd better treat the whole visible church with some kind of respect!

A few years ago the battles were hot between this Council and that, and we had our guns trained on what might have been our brothers, instead of on Satan, our true enemy. God's angel will one day sickle out the tares from the wheat, but in the meantime, let's be careful how we handle even the visible church. You may not decide to attend a certain one, but you don't have to take potshots at it.

Think about how Jesus identifies with the church. Here was Paul, on the road to Damascus. He thought he'd only been giving *Christians* a hard time, but when he said, "Who art Thou, Lord?" Jesus answered "I am Jesus, *whom you are persecuting.*"

To persecute a brother is to persecute Jesus. To speak roughly of a brother is to speak roughly of Jesus. To touch His disciples is to touch Him!

Discipling One Another

*W*hy is the church second in priority only to God Himself?

1. Because it preexisted in the heart of God before the world began (Eph. 1:4). This is said of no other of God's institutions—the government, the family, or anything else.

2. Because the church is Christ's gift to the Father (Eph.1:11, 18). What does God get out of it, to have sent His Son to die on the cross? He gets us! And—hallelujah—he thinks that's wonderful!

3. Because the church is Christ's Body (Eph. 1:22–23). The church is His "fullness," His completion. In a truer way than Eve ever completed Adam, we complete Christ. He has put in His plan an absolute necessity for us. In a genuine sense, the church is not an organization but an organism.

4. Because the church is convincing evidence to the universe that God is merciful, good, and wise (Eph. 3:9–10); and this demonstration is throughout all space and all time.

Oh, Christian, love the church! God does!

Discipling One Another

To him be glory in the church and in Christ Jesus throughout all generations, for ever and ever! Amen. (Eph. 3:21)

*J*ohn 17 is a long discussion by God the Son with God the Father. (How self-revealing God is!) And when God talks with God, what are His godly, all-encompassing concerns? There are basically three:

1. John 17:1–5: *the glory of the Father and the glory of the Son.*

2. John 17:6–19: *the well-being of believers*—their protection, their unity, their joy, their sanctification. . . . How He loves us!

3. John 17:20–26: *the salvation of the world*—that others will believe, that they will know God yearns for them!

Do you want to move into the heart of God? Do you want to be "in sync" with Him, sharing His own priorities? In John 15, just before Jesus went to the cross, He communicated these same three priorities among His final commands to His eleven disciples. And they're for you and for me as well:

1. *Make your chief concern the glory of the Father and the glory of the Son*, through the power of the Spirit. Be zealous above all to put Him first, first, first! Move away from all competition with His firstness; settle into Him. As He said, "Remain in me" (John 15:1–11). That's your first priority.

2. *Share His concern for the well-being of your fellow believers*—their protection, their unity, their joy, their sanctification. Give your time, your gifts, yourself! As Jesus said, "Love each other" (John 15:12–17). That's your second priority.

3. *Share His concern for this needy world*; reach out! As He said, "You also must testify, for you have been with me from the beginning" (John 15:18–27). That's your third priority, your third area of concern.

So, here in John 17, take off your shoes. You're on holy ground. Sit at Jesus' feet. Learn His thinking. And give all you are to share His concerns, love His loves, accomplish His purposes.

Women's Devotional Bible

241

*T*he three priorities [Christ, His body, the world for which He died] are such a practical part of my life now that they even affect my daily list of things to do. Often I come to a point in the day when I have choices: what's most important of the things left to be done?

If I'm guided in my "to do" list by these three priorities, then the important takes precedence over the urgent. That's so necessary! If we live always doing the urgent, we spend our time responding to alarm bells and racing to put out fires. Ten years later we'll feel totally impoverished, because over the long haul the seemingly urgent is seldom important.

Take a good look at your life. Whatever kind of woman you are—wife, mother, career woman, single parent—have you got your priorities in order? Are you building a life of eternal consequences?

If not, like a good sculptor, you need to do some strong, radical gouging and reshaping to start making the large mass of your remaining life what you—and God—want it to be.

Disciplines of the Beautiful Woman

So that in everything [Christ] might have the supremacy. (Col. 1:18)

As God's chosen people, holy and dearly loved, clothe yourselves with compassion, kindness, humility, gentleness and patience. Bear with each other and forgive whatever grievances you may have against one another. Forgive as the Lord forgave you. (Col. 3:12, 13)

Be wise in the way you act toward outsiders; make the most of every opportunity. (Col. 4:5)

Seek first his kingdom. (Matt. 6:33)

*L*ive your life, not doing things from moment to moment because you feel like it, but doing things decided on in advance because it's the time you set to do them.

Manage your life; don't let it manage you—blown here and there by every little wind that comes along.

Employ the principle of firsts:

"I have only so much time every day. I believe the Bible is more important than the newspaper; therefore I will read the Bible *first*."

"I believe helping my neighbor is more important than this crossword puzzle; therefore I will help my neighbor *first*."

Lace needs holes as well as thread. But build into your life a planned pattern of thread first, and the holes will take care of themselves.

Music needs rests as well as notes. But build into your life a planned rhythm of notes first, and the rests will fall naturally into their places.

Make your life beautiful with planned, regular disciplines.

You Don't Have to Quit

He who ignores discipline despises himself. (Prov. 15:32)

𝒲hen I first bought a notebook and organized it into sections, no one had suggested it to me. I didn't do it because it was going to be some great new beginning in my life. I can't even remember actually getting it.

Over the ensuing months I began leaning on my notebook more and more for daily living, seeing what it could do. Fortunately it was brown and just Bible-size, so it was easy to get the habit of going out the door with Bible, notebook, and purse.

After several years of literally living out of it, hesitantly, very hesitantly, I shared it one time at a women's conference. *Whammo!* It went off like a bombshell. Scores told me they were going home to buy notebooks. I shared it at other conferences, and the feedback began. I'd hear the words "It's changed my life. . . ."

As your notebook*is filled with that which is most meaningful in every area of your total life, and as you learn to use it continuously through each day, you'll:

1. Stay on target in your living;

2. Become more prayerful;

3. Be more deeply impressed by God's truths;

4. Keep your mind filled with the pure, the beautiful;

5. Not forget what you're supposed to do!

Disciplines of the Beautiful Woman

Be very careful, then, how you live—not as unwise but as wise, making the most of every opportunity, because the days are evil. Therefore do not be foolish, but understand what the Lord's will is. (Eph. 5:15–17)

---

*If you want to consider living your life by a notebook, write to me for a brochure at Renewal Ministries, 4500 Campus Drive, Suite 662, Newport Beach, California 92660.

Make every effort to add to your faith goodness, . . . knowledge, . . . self-control, . . . perseverance, . . . godliness, . . . brotherly kindness, and . . . love" (2 Pet. 1:5–7).

"Add to your faith": Supplement it, flesh it out. Being a Christian doesn't mean believing and then just sitting around. Now that you have faith in God's part, make every effort— that's your part.

That's disciplines.

That's regular "holy habits."

That's pacing yourself for the cross-country run to your future.

Says Henri Nouwen, "A spiritual life without discipline is impossible." Tighten your belt. Get tough on yourself. GOFORIT.

A woman once said to the great Paderewski, "Sir, you are truly a genius."

"Well," he answered, "before I was a genius, I was a drudge!"

To get there, to win—your life needs discipline, order, and arrangement.

"If one examines the secret behind a championship football team, a magnificent orchestra, or a successful business, the principle ingredient is invariably discipline."*

You will only
discover excellence
on the other side
of hard work

You Don't Have to Quit

---

*James Dobson, quoted in *Disciplines of the Home*.

$\mathcal{F}$or you to rest—that is, to live in total acceptance of God's way—demands quiet.

I don't mean a "quiet time," a period for Bible study and prayer, preceded by and followed by the old frantic rat race. Doing that gives your brain mixed signals; it breeds confusion; it gives you a grey life.

Resting demands quiet *all the time*. However active your external life may be, He wants you to develop between your two ears, in the discipline of your heart, a lifelong attitude of rest in Him.

To rest in God permanently means to hand over each activity, each situation of your life, to Him and to learn the habit of trusting Him to *work for you*.

To guard your inner life, you must guard your outer life. How's your pace? Are you too busy? Says 1 Thessalonians 4:11, "Make it your ambition to lead a quiet life."

Disciplines of the Heart

Your beauty should not come from outward adornment, such as braided hair and the wearing of gold jewelry and fine clothes. Instead, it should be that of your inner self, the unfading beauty of a gentle and quiet spirit. (1 Pet. 3:3–4)

*T*he discipline of solitude is different from your quiet time, but one that will greatly help it.

It's not that as soon as we get alone with God, we are prepared to hear Him speak. A slot of time is not all that we need. Says Henri Nouwen,

> We are usually surrounded by so much inner and outer noise, it is hard to truly hear our God when he is speaking to us. . . .
>
> A spiritual discipline is necessary in order to move slowly . . . to an obedient life, from a life filled with noisy worries to a life in which there is some free inner space. . . .*

Your soul desperately needs aloneness and silence. (A person who's always available isn't worth much when he *is* available.)

Maybe at first you won't be able to stand more than five to ten minutes a day, but make sure it is absolutely *daily*. Be totally alone. Have the television and radio off, take the phone off its hook, close doors if the traffic blares outside, make your atmosphere as quiet and undistracting as possible. Read no books. Do nothing "useful."

When you've gotten rid of your outer distractions, you may become very aware of your inner distractions—the anxieties, the bad memories, the angers, the chaos of your heart. Maybe for a few weeks your solitude will not only seem a waste, but even painful.

But persevere with this discipline! Be deliberately quiet. As neither outer nor inner distractions are fed and attended to, they will gradually withdraw. But you won't become empty, you'll become aware of God and eternity and your stripped-down, quieted, unfolding self.

You Don't Have to Quit

---

*Making All Things New.

*W*here can you go for solitude? "Jesus often withdrew to lonely places and prayed" (Luke 5:16). In a city, lonely places are hard to find. We live by the ocean, and Ray knows stretches of beach where few people go. There he talks to and listens to God.

Find a closet; find a spot behind your house; find a hiding place. Incessant sound will dull you, desensitize you. You were made for quiet. The silent forces are the great forces: sunbeams, gravity, dew. There is strength in aloneness, in listening, in observing, in prayer.

"Be still, and know that I am God," He says (Ps. 46:10). In your kind of world, full of noise pollution, *listen, in the disciplines of your heart, to the still, small voice of God.*

Elijah stood at the mouth of a mountain cave, and along came a wind so violent it shattered rocks—

> But the LORD was not in the wind. After the wind there was an earthquake, but the LORD was not in the earthquake. After the earthquake came a fire, but the LORD was not in the fire. And after the fire came a gentle whisper [a still, small voice]. When Elijah heard it, he pulled his cloak over his face. (1 Kings 19:11–13)

Oh, the holiness of that moment! I think Elijah pulled his cloak across to humble himself, but also to shut out every other sound.

Some of our foremothers just threw their aprons up over their heads.

Tune out . . . and tune in.

Disciplines of the Heart

*W*hat does it mean to "enter into God's rest," as Hebrews 4 tells you? It means cutting from your life everything that is of the flesh, purely for self, and surrendering yourself to let God work through you every good work that He wants to do. That's His kind of rest.

Be rested, then. Be rested. Don't let any seemingly good thing keep you from being rested.

It will take the discipline of your heart to shift down. For a while you'll feel restless, guilty that you're not "doing" something every minute. You'll want to "get busy," maintain the former pace, rectify every situation by your own nervous efforts. Who said it would be easy? *"Make every effort* to enter into that rest" (Heb. 4:11).

But if you do learn to slow down, before long you'll know yourself better. You'll know the ones you live with better. And you'll have become a little island of poise in a mixed-up world. Your family, according to whatever measure of control and influence you still have, may become one less candidate for divorce, drugs, tragedy.

And you will say by your very lifestyle that you have time for life and for God—that He is the active One, working in you that which is well pleasing in His sight.

Disciplines of the Heart

The LORD your God is with you.
    he is mighty to save.
He will take great delight in you,
    he will quiet you with his love,
    he will rejoice over you with singing. (Zeph. 3:17)

*I*t's Friday, but Sunday's coming!" Have you thought about why, in the overarching "modes of operations" of God, Sunday is the first day of the week?

God's strategy is silence, then action; waiting or resting, then work. Have you noticed it?

When in Genesis 1 He created twenty-four hour days, He made them "the evening and the morning." First you slept, then you worked. The mind frame was not that you work and then drop into bed exhausted to recuperate. You slept first and did your work in the stance of "restedness."

Quiet, then action.

Take when the Israelites finally arrived at the border of their Promised Land. Did they just tumble into it pell-mell and start to occupy? No, they had three days of rest and quiet, to get their orders, to think, to be totally "together" and ready.

Think about the book of Acts, which means "book of action." You have twenty-seven chapters of fast-paced traveling, witnessing, establishing chuches, and so on. But there are twenty-eight chapters in the book! That's right. The first chapter is dead, boulevard stop. Preceding all the action you have a chapter of quiet, of rest, of prayer, of waiting on God.

The morning of the first day of the week—that's when we rise and worship Him. What a perfect way to prepare for the week to come!

Don't think of it as "hype" time.

It's for listening, worshiping, waiting, and silence.

Every week it's the way you get poised and ready for living.

Up with Worship

$\mathcal{L}$et me suggest a twofold plan of attack for you, to keep your heart-attitude right.

Number one: See yourself *as God sees you:* a little child of eternity, moldable and pliable. Number two: Surrender yourself totally under His hands. Confess your faults, your sins, and let God powerfully rework your life.

The proud, the "adults" of this world, the people who think by their own efforts they have it all together—or can get it all together—God resists. He works against them. He makes them stumble. He puts holes in their pockets. He hassles them. He opposes them.

The Old and New Testaments say it together in chorus: "He mocks proud mockers *but gives grace to the humble*" (Prov. 3:34, emphasis added; see also James 4:6).

A little child is humble. He's not hardened yet—not sophisticated; he's impressionable; he's moldable.

Jesus said, "I tell you the truth, unless you change and become like little children, you will never enter the kingdom of heaven." And He pulled a little one next to Him right then, and He said, "Therefore, whoever humbles himself like this child is the greatest in the kingdom of heaven" (Matt. 18:3–4).

God calls His own His "children," and that's what He wants us to be: not childish, but childlike. The values of being childlike are immense: You'll be forever teachable, dependent, and trusting—uncorrupted and uncynical. You won't "crust over" and harden, so you can be always growing and discovering and changing and improving.

God will watch over childlike people; says Psalm 116:6, "The LORD protects the simplehearted."

Children Are Wet Cement

> Alas, and did my Saviour bleed?
>   And did my Sov'reign die?
> Would He devote that sacred head
>   For such a worm as I?
>
>   —*Isaac Watts*

God's great men have often confessed that they were small and unworthy. (See, for instance, Judges 6:15–16; 1 Samuel 15:17; 1 Samuel 18:18, 23; 1 Kings 3:7–10—there are many more.) Don't worry, they weren't groveling around with poor self-images; they were great because they were humble. And God could afford to exalt them because all the glory and credit remained His.

"Therefore," said Paul, who was such a great apostle, "I will boast all the more gladly about my weaknesses, so that Christ's power may rest on me" (2 Cor. 12:9).

That seems going too far. How could he "boast gladly about his weaknesses"? Because he understood how gladly God forgives! He knew that when we rush to God with our confessions, God rushes to us with His forgiveness! It's like the prodigal son turning homeward—and the father running to meet him.

I'm learning in my own life that constant, instant confession is the means to continual health, to unbroken communion with the Lord and with others. As often and as quickly as I say "I'm sorry," God or the offended ones say, "That's okay!"

And when I keep short accounts on my sins with continual confessions, then acknowledging my sins doesn't crush my ego and totally embarrass me. I can open up gladly about my weaknesses—and expect glad forgiveness!

Joanna: A Story of Renewal

*A*while back, Ray preached on Mark 14:3. "Here came Mary," he said, "with her alabaster vase of nard to the dinner where Jesus was. She broke the bottle and poured it on Him."

An alabaster vase—milky white, veined, smooth, precious. And pure nard inside! Gone forever. According to John 12:3, the whole house became filled with the fragrance.

The need for Christians everywhere (nobody is exempt) is to be broken. The vase has to be smashed! *Of course* it's awkward and scary to be broken! *Of course* it's easier to keep up that cold, alabaster front.

It was costly for Mary, too.

When Ray preached on Mark 14:3, I wrote on a card, "Lord, break my strong will, my argumentativeness, my quickness to reach decisions ahead of others and always think I'm right, my desire to have my opinion always considered. I'm sure I'm often obnoxious, Lord—maybe embarrassing to Ray. Forgive me, and help my fervent spirit be converted into just being fervent in loving You, fervent in joy, fervent in peace, *et cetera.* Lord, break me. Thank You for doing it! Amen."

> The high and lofty one who inhabits eternity, the Holy One, says this: "I live in that high and holy place where those with contrite, humble spirits dwell; and I refresh the humble and give new courage to those with repentant hearts" (Isa. 57:15 TLB).

The way to up is down!
The holy One lives among broken people!

Up with Worship

If we confess our sins, he is faithful and just and will forgive us our sins and purify us from all unrighteousness. If we claim we have not sinned, we make him out to be a liar and his word has no place in our lives. (1 John 1:9–10)

*W*e can easily confess the sins of others. All those awful people out there in America, or elsewhere, need revival. This attitude makes fussing Christians ("America is going down the tubes"), and it purges nobody's sins at all.

"Don't grumble against each other, brothers," says James 5:9, "or you will be judged. The Judge is standing at the door!"

David expressed the only attitude which God promises to honor: "Cleanse *me* . . . wash *me*" (Ps. 51:7, emphasis added).

Yesterday I said some things on the phone to our daughter Sherry that I need not have said. She took it as an unjust criticism, and immediately we had a problem. The rest of the phone conversation was definitely unhappy, and I hung up groaning. For a while I rammed around town, doing errands and feeling miserable. Then I knew what I had to do.

I bought a basket of pink chrysanthemums. I showed up at Sherry's front door, looking and feeling foolish. I ate dirt. I apologized for my big mouth. I only wish I'd thought of one other touch: to put a card in the flowers saying, "Single-handedly, I have fought my way into this hopeless mess!"

After hugs and tears came a glass of iced tea and some fun, and all was well again. *Whew! Relief!* Now I can look Sherry in the eye again and know we're still best friends: "Therefore confess your sins to each other and pray for each other so that you may be healed" (James 5:16).

Joanna: A Story of Renewal

*I*t's just plain smart, then, to confess. When I defend myself, others will be quick to judge me. When I judge myself, others won't—I got there first (Rom. 14:10–13).

In a forest fire there's a place the flames don't touch; it's the place that the fire has already burned! The fire's already done everything it could do, and therefore that spot is actually a place of protection and safety.

Our confessions are what firefighters call "backfiring," deliberately burning an area in advance before the fire can get to it. We protect ourselves when we confess! We are agreeing with others' potential—and correct—judgment of us, and then, from that moment on, we can never be justly accused again. Before judgment fire got to us, we jumped in and confessed!

Oh, this is a good word for me, struggling toward godliness! I love it. It makes me happy. Listen to this great word written centuries ago by Francis de Sales in that ancient classic, *Introduction to a Devout Life*:

> Let us not be disturbed at the sight of our imperfections, for *perfection consists in fighting against them*. And how can we fight against them without seeing them, or overcome them without encountering them? *Our victory consists not in being insensible to them, but in refusing them our consent*; now to be displeased with them is not to consent to them. . . .
>
> *We shall always be victorious provided we do but fight*. (emphases added)

Joanna: A Story of Renewal

This is the victory that has overcome the world, even our faith. (1 John 5:4)

Sin shall not be your master. (Rom. 6:14)

For what is our hope, our joy, or the crown in which we will glory in the presence of our Lord Jesus when he comes? Is it not you? Indeed, you are our glory and joy. (1 Thess. 2:19–20)

God's beautiful family members are waiting to be loved. They're all around you. They're lonely. They're hungry to know the Bible and grow, to be given time, to be patted and hugged and laughed with and cried with and counseled. They, too, want you, yourself! Nothing less will do.

And, oh, my friend, isn't it amazing that some day Jesus will even say, "Truly I say to you, to the extent that you did it to one of these brothers of Mine, even the least of them, you did it to Me" (Matt. 25:40 NASB)?

"You loved the members of my family—you loved Me. For them you inconvenienced yourself; you went without, to complete their material needs; you entered into My sufferings in order to fill them full; for them you endured hassle and strain— and your greatest joy was their maturity and completion. You shared My goals for them!

"Thank you! Well done! Enter into your rewards (did you dream they would be this wonderful?)! You make Me so happy. Don't you understand now why, on My part, the cross was worth it all? Even the least saint is so precious!

"Let Me give you another hug. You loved My family—you loved Me. It wasn't easy; I know. I watched you every moment, and I interceded for you, that you would persevere. . . .

"And you did! I'm filled with exceeding joy. You identified with My sufferings; you were willing! Oh, My dear one!

"Come. We've both suffered; now let's go celebrate together." . . .

Discipling One Another

*I*n Matthew 28:18–20, Jesus' parting words told us to go disciple others, teaching them everything that he has taught us.

That's what immediately began to happen ten days later, in Acts 2:41 and following. And later it became Paul's lifestyle, and he told his disciples to do the same: "[Timothy], the things which you have heard from me in the presence of many witnesses, these entrust to faithful men, who will be able to teach others also" (2 Tim. 2:2 NASB).

This is basic, biblical Christianity. No Christian service can substitute for this: not directing the church choir, not ushering, not cooking church dinners—not even writing Christian books. Discipling is foundational; it keeps you in touch with God and with people, and keeps you bringing the two together. It keeps you growing in grace: Your personality is challenged and stretched. It keeps you growing in knowledge: You automatically keep learning God's Word. It's God's plan for your life.

Have you been a Christian for a while and learned a few things? *Then you're responsible to act out your role as a spiritual father or mother in God's family*. Gather a few around you and say, "Let's meet for Bible study and pray and share our lives— say, till next June. What do you think?"

Or are you a "young" Christian who doesn't know much yet? *You're responsible to act out your role as a child in the family*. Go to someone you respect and say, "I really want to learn more about the Bible and about the Christian life. Would you take me on for a while and disciple me?"

So that you won't ever stagnate, there should always be a "flow" through your life. You should always be learning from those who know more than you do, and you should always be teaching those who know less.

Yes, all of us are forever responsible to "put it together" in the family of God!

Discipling One Another

*W*hat happens when people are "born again" into God's family? Grown men, able women, important people recognized for their skills and status, have to have the courage to step over into God's family and play a brand-new role: they're a new "little spiritual brother or sister" with much to learn.

The parents and big brothers and sisters in God's family must be willing to assume their roles. They must give him plenty of time, feeding information, tenderly rebuking, pointing out Scriptures, and simply reacting to life in front of him so that he can learn how Christians react to life. . . . They must do and be everything that's needed to bring that spiritual baby, through the power of the Holy Spirit, to maturity.

But if Christians don't see the functions of the members of the family of God, they won't see each other with spiritual eyes. They won't see a newly converted "big shot" as a new baby brother. They'll simply see him as a "big shot," and he'll be encouraged to talk too much and not listen enough. Then he'll be cheated and his growth stunted.

In God's family we play completely different roles from those the world knows. And it's essential that we understand them and that we function, in order to help each other grow strong in Christ.

Discipling One Another

Instead, speaking the truth in love, we will in all things grow up into him who is the Head, that is, Christ. From him the whole body, joined and held together by every supporting ligament, grows and builds itself up in love, as each part does its work. (Eph. 4:15–16)

$\mathcal{W}$e've learned a lot in recent years about the church's being the Body of Christ, and, thinking about hands and feet and eyes and mouths, we've sought to discover our gifts and function with them. That's one picture of the church, and a wonderful one, and we praise God for this rediscovery of truth.

But that concept isn't all. If we know only this kind of "Body" life, we've left lots of single adults standing awkwardly around the scene without family. We have numberless teenagers from non-Christian homes who have no spiritual parents to guide them and who get all their wisdom from their own peers in the youth group—poor Timothys without Pauls! We have lonely widows and widowers, and other former wives and husbands floating around like second-class citizens—because we tend to think mostly "physical family," and to make our churches couples-oriented and physical-family-oriented.

But that's not the *"ecclesia"*! The called-out ones come from every possible broken-family situation; and not until we see ourselves as functioning first as a spiritual family will we all draw together and meet each others' needs.

We can't organize this; but we must teach it and learn it well, and then let the Holy Spirit make it happen. It comes out of a deep understanding of "priority two"—and a deep commitment to each other, our beautiful forever-family of God.

Discipling One Another

Do not rebuke an older man harshly, but exhort him as if he were your father. Treat younger men as brothers, older women as mothers, and younger women as sisters, with absolute purity. (1 Tim. 5:1–2)

I've been assigned the specific role of temporary mother to two kids: a white boy and a black girl.

Cathy was in one of my small groups, and her high school son was keeping his distance. "Cathy," I said, "let me lend a hand in mothering your child." We both knew this may be a part of putting our lives together, to be available to each other's kids. When Jonathan and David made a covenant of friendship, it was to include responsibility for their children (1 Sam. 20:15–16; 2 Sam. 9).

I invited Cathy's son out for a Coke date. Wonder of wonders, he accepted! Over the weeks we shared our lives together, and I poured out some of my troubles to him, and he poured out to me his girlfriend troubles, his parent troubles, his frustrations. We giggled together, and we talked seriously together. After a few months, with no pushing from me, he'd decided his girl was the wrong one for him (he was right), and he was praying out loud with me, and he'd rejoined the church youth group to make some new friends. When his mother reported he was hugging her in the kitchen, I knew my job was over.

Patty was the daughter of another of my dear friends, and Patty was going through the inevitable confusion, as a black high schooler in a mostly white church, of finding out who she was. Oh, how my heart went out to her—so beautiful, and with so much potential.

Some of our Coke dates were stormy—but today?

I have a lunch date with Patty coming up. By now she's a grown, poised, glamorous woman launched into a career, and what turns her on most of all is Jesus, and praising Him, and witnessing of Him. I'm honored to be her friend.

The world is full of struggling, hurting kids. Why don't you start "mothering" one?

Discipling One Another

*O*h, my friend! If you could understand what He's done for you—and what He's doing—and what He will yet do!

As Isaiah 63:1–10 explains it, Jesus Christ our Lord,
Dismayed over the death-sins in which we're totally—and willingly—enmeshed,
Feeling intensely the loneliness and rejection of being the only One who cares enough to do something about it,
Dons His soldier's garb and takes sword in hand and comes down to do what He knows, for love's sake, He must do.
He battles us sinners to the death—His death—becoming totally bloody and ruined and eternally stained and scarred—
For what?
To rescue the very ones He's battling—to rescue us, His enemies, whom He loves so passionately—to rescue the ones who fight Him, bloody Him, hurt Him, defeat Him, wound and kill Him,
To rescue us so that He can rise, scarred and bloodied, to enfold us tenderly to His breast and gently clear our vision so we can see how deeply He loves us, and then to spend eternity pouring out His kindness upon the precious ones He's rescued, comforting us and sustaining us and doing uncounted good things for us all the days of our eternal lives.
Alleluia!

Disciplines of the Heart

> Yet it was the LORD's will to crush him and cause
> him to suffer. . . .
>> The will of the LORD will prosper in his hand.
> After the suffering of his soul,
>> he will see the light of life and be satisfied.
>> *(Isa. 53:10–11)*

Out of the ivory palaces into a world of woe;
Only His great, eternal love made my Saviour go.

$\mathcal{H}$e had always, eternally, been alive and active. "In the beginning was the Word," says John 1:1—reaching back beyond creation, before Genesis 1:1!

Just as His death was not the end of Him, so His birth was not the beginning of Him.*

He was God. And yet He came to this world and

made himself nothing, . . .
being made in human likeness. (Phil. 2: 6–7)

Incredible! He created everything—and then He voluntarily submitted to His own creation! He became tired and thirsty, just like one of us.

Before, He'd been so furious against sin that He refused at first to lead His people into the Promised Land: He said they were so rebellious, He "might destroy [them] on the way" (Exod. 33:3).

Yet descending to earth in His incarnation, He stooped so far down that *He meekly asked a prostitute for a drink of water.*

Truly, profoundly, *"he humbled himself"* (Phil. 2:8).

Fix Your Eyes on Jesus

The Faces of Jesus.

*J*esus spent six times as long working as a carpenter as He did in full-time ministry. And I want to tell you—*it was a good thing He didn't shrink from all those laborious, tedious carpenter-years as His preparation.* Once the ministry began,

> Never in human history were human frame and nervous system to be called on to endure such unremitting strain. . . . Only a physically perfect constitution could have supported such unceasing activity and expenditure of nervous force. . . .
>
> His recorded journeys during the three years covered at least two thousand five hundred miles on foot, frequently surrounded by crowds, and always teaching, preaching, healing.
>
> And what better preparation than twelve hours a day spent in the sawpit or at the bench, planing and hammering? These silent years . . . were invaluable in building up the physical and nervous reserves which were to be so heavily overdrawn in coming days that He would stagger under the weight of His cross."*

Jesus—pale, puffy-eyed, and effeminate, as in some of our paintings? No way. He was a "man's man."

Now in heaven there is a Man at the Father's right hand! And He's as manly as ever—*as human as ever*—having become the glorious Human that Adam started out to be and lost, and that we soon shall be. "And just as we have borne the likeness of the earthly man [Adam], so shall we bear the likeness of the man from heaven [Christ]." (1 Cor. 15:49)

I can hardly wait, can you?

Fix Your Eyes on Jesus

---

*Oswald Sanders: *Christ Incomparable*.

*J*esus was a man—but *don't ever forget He was and is God.*

> He is the image of the invisible God, the firstborn over
> all creation. For by him all things were created, . . . by him
> and for him. He is before all things, and in him all things
> hold together. . . . God was pleased to have all his fullness
> dwell in him. (Col. 1:15–17, 19)

In Zechariah 13:6 and 7, God the Father calls the Messiah
His "Associate," His Fellow, His Equal.

In Isaiah 40:10 Christ is called "Jehovah," a name so glorious the Hebrews left out its vowels—"YHWH," making it
unpronounceable. And whenever a scribe copying Scriptures
wrote out that name, he would first wipe his pen and dip it in
fresh ink.

This is our Holy One, Jesus Christ the Lord, the Son of God.

When Peter called Him this—"the Christ, the Son of the
living God"—Jesus answered, "Blessed are you" (Matt. 16:16–
17).

John told all his readers it was the reason he wrote his book:

> that you may believe that Jesus is the Christ, the Son of God,
> and that by believing you may have life in his name. (John
> 20:31)

Is your heart right now bowed in acknowledgement?

> *A prayer:* Lord, I say with Job,
>   "My ears had heard of you
>   but now my eyes have seen you." (Job 42:5)
> And I say with Thomas,
>   "My Lord and my God!" (John 20:28)

Fix Your Eyes on Jesus

*T*he Lord is in His holy house"—Oh, grace
　　　　beyond describing,
That Christ in me should please to dwell—
　　　　Immanuel residing!
"My soul doth magnify the Lord," I sing with lowly Mary,
That God should choose to enter in
　　This
　　　　humble sanctuary!

Not now in little Bethlehem, As in the tender story;
Not now upon a mercy seat, The bright *Shekinah* glory,
But in the body of His saint, He maketh His residing,
Both He in me and I in Him
　　In
　　　　fellowship abiding.

Within my heart a burning bush, Within, a
　　　　mountain smoking;
This flesh of mine a temple veil, The wondrous
　　　　Presence cloaking;
Within this broken earthenware A high and holy
　　　　treasure:
Oh, mystery of mysteries!
　　Oh, grace
　　　　beyond all measure!

"The Lord is in His Holy house"—Mysterious
　　　　habitation!
I feel His presence here within And offer my
　　　　oblation.
Keep burning, incense of my soul! Keep
　　　　cleansing me, O Laver!
I want to serve and praise my God
　　Forever
　　　　and forever!

　　　　　　　　　　　—Anne Ortlund

　　　　　　　　Women's Devotional Bible

Let God give you a view, a vision, of your future. Only at that point will you know what to do and what not to do—how to "eliminate and concentrate"!

Renoir, the great French impressionistic painter, at one point suffered total paralysis in his legs. For two years a doctor worked on them to help Renoir walk again.

At last the famous painter stood and actually walked across the room. Then he surrendered to his invalid chair, for life. "I give up," he said. "It takes all my will power, and I would have nothing left for painting."

Renoir's biographer, his own son Jean, says that from then on, his paintings were "a display of fireworks to the end. . . . freed from all theories, from all fears"!*

Wrote Andrew Murray,

And now, who is ready to enter into this New and everlasting Covenant with his whole heart? Let each of us do it.

Begin by asking God very humbly to give you, by the Spirit who dwells in you, the vision of the heavenly life of wholehearted love and obedience, as it has actually been prepared for you in Christ. It is an existing reality, a spiritual endowment out of the life of God which can come upon you. . . .

Ask earnestly, definitely, believingly, that God can reveal this to you. Rest not till you know fully what your Father means you to be, and has provided for your most certainly being.

When you begin to see [it]. . . . offer yourself to God unreservedly to be taken up into it.†

For your life, look beyond, beyond . . . And picture it as clearly as you can . . . Until faith becomes literal sight.

        You Don't Have to Quit

---

*Quoted in the *Los Angeles Times*, 16 March 1985.
†Andrew Murray, *The Two Covenants*.

*T*hink future! Live each day so that later on you'll look back with satisfaction.

You can do that! You can't manage your circumstances, but you can manage *how you react* to your circumstances. Remember, living is between your ears!

So from this moment on, God helping you, if you choose you can do two things to leave behind good footprints.

1. Start building for yourself the memories you want when you look back tomorrow.

2. Start building, as well, other people's memories of you. For instance, *speak your negative words, but write your positive ones.*

Think future! When you're dead and gone, you want to leave behind in this world not one bad piece of paper for people to find—but hundreds of good ones for them to remember you by.

Live so they'll cry at your funeral. Wouldn't you like someday to be really missed? Then "reach out and touch." Each smile of yours, each hug, each encouraging word could become a specific little memory in someone's mind later on.

When you spend your life with future rewards in mind, your present life becomes rewarding as well. Build your own future memories, and build other people's future memories of you.

Walk *so you leave behind good footprints.*

You Don't Have to Quit

I pray also that the eyes of your heart may be enlightened in order that you may know the hope to which he has called you. (Eph. 1:18)

*D*o you know how you sculpt an elephant? It's easy: you just get a large rock and cut away everything that doesn't look like an elephant.

Don't laugh, there's a great truth here. You may look at your life with all its activities and interests, some of importance and some clutter, and it looks to you like a huge, unwieldy mass—a big rock—with little potential for getting through your troubles to a life that wins.

But when you have "visualized," when your heart has been enlightened, when you have pictured mentally what God is calling you to be and therefore what *you* want to be, then you can methodically start cutting away everything that doesn't contribute to that.

That's your need: a dream for your life, the vision that God will give you. And when you begin to see its shape you'll think, "Well, certainly *this* activity isn't compatible, and probably *that* ought to go. . . ."

And you'll say, "If I'm going to be this in my future, then I need to prepare myself these days by this, this, and *this*. "Eliminate and concentrate! Live your present life building toward your wonderful future!

You Don't Have to Quit

I urge you to live a life worthy of the calling you have received. (Eph. 4:1)

$\mathcal{M}$any people live their lives only as the sum total of all the imprints made upon them when they were young and impressionable. Those people are the ones who refuse to be worked on and remade by God's powerful, reshaping grace.

I didn't tell you the best part of the story; I saved it for the last. I'm a new person! And so can you be a new person.

Even little Betty Ann Sweet's name got changed. Mother dropped the "Betty," and I put an E on "Ann." And then I lost the name "Sweet" when I married Ray Ortlund.

How did I get changed? I accepted Jesus Christ into my heart and life, to be my Savior from all my sins and fears, and to rework me into whatever shape He desired.

And all by Himself, He implanted into me a reciprocal love for Himself. Anne Ortlund loves the Lord! That's the strongest, most driving force of my life. I know it. It powerfully shapes, controls and motivates the little Betty Ann inside of me. It works—no, not *it* but *He*—works constantly seeking to win over my basic tendencies to hide, to sleep too long, to show off, to be hasty, to lie, to procrastinate, to be dull, to hang back . . . and a thousand more of Betty Ann's characteristics.

The Holy Spirit lures me on, making me pursue Him more, love harder, laugh more, work longer. He makes me impatient with meaninglessness, with waste, with vulgarity.

I love to live in eternity. The caverns of conceiving and pursuing and achieving are arched so high over my head that I am lost below. Yet I have a conviction that I will expand to inhabit them all before I'm done. I'll fly! I'll soar! God is so vast, and God is drawing me on. God is so vast—but He loves me, and He's laughing as He tugs at me.

Betty Ann Sweet is fading more and more. My sin has been dealt with, forgiven, and forgotten. Not often do I wring those little hands; I reach them up to Him, and to *up*. Whatever the future is, for me it is up.

Children Are Wet Cement

269

*W*hether mother or not, wife or not, you're a woman—wonderful, unique. And even if you're paralyzed from the neck down, you can be God's beautiful woman. His Holy Spirit within you can give you all the self-discipline you need to focus your attention on Him, not yourself, to adore Him for large chunks of time, to think of His attributes, to confess your sins to Him and experience all the ways which involve life's "top priority" and which concern your central core, the real you. You have every resource to become one of His beautiful women, and to be a great influence on those around you and around the world.

The timing of your life is also unique. It was time for you to read this book. Opportunity, they say, is like a horse. It gallops up to you from nowhere, and pauses. Now it's time to get on. If you don't, he'll soon be gone, and the clatter of his hoofs will be heard dying away in the distance.

Yes, you're a woman—handmade by God to fulfill wonderful plans of His. Do you feel a time-release capsule exploding inside you, urging you to new interests, new opportunities, new horizons?

Is it total revolution for you?

Write me and tell me about it.

Love,

Anne Ortlund
4500 Campus Drive, Suite 662
Newport Beach, California 92660

Disciplines of the Beautiful Woman

Bibliography

Arndt and Gingrich, eds. *Greek-English Lexicon of the New Testament*. Chicago: University of Chicago Press, 1957.

Briscoe, Stuart. *The Fullness of Christ*. Grand Rapids, Mich.: Zondervan, 1965.

Bueckner, Frederick. *The Faces of Jesus*. 1974. Reprint. New York: Stearn/Harper and Row, 1989.

Clark, James M., ed. *Meister Eckhart*. London: Thomas Nelson and Sons, 1957.

The Cloud of Unknowing, a version in modern English of a fourteenth-century classic. New York: Harper and Brothers, 1948.

Daily Walk Magazine. Walk Through the Bible Ministries, P.O. Box 80587, Atlanta, Georgia 30366.

de Sales, Francis. *Introduction to a Devout Life*. Cleveland, N.Y.: World, 1952.

Dimnet, Ernest. *The Art of Thinking*. Reprint. Greenwich, Conn.: Fawcett, 1928.

Dunnam, Maxie. *The Workbook of Spiritual Disciplines*. Nashville: Upper Room, 1984.

Eller, Vernard. *The Simple Life*. Grand Rapids, Mich: Eerdmans, 1973.

Foley, W. Ross. *You Can Win Over Weariness*. Glendale, Calif.: Regal, 1977.

Hefley, James. *Life Changes*. Wheaton, Ill.: Tyndale House, 1984.

Henry, Carl. "The Road to Eternity." *Christianity Today*, 17 July 1981, 32.

Howard, Thomas. "Who Am I? Who Am I?" *Christianity Today*, 8 July 1977, 12–13.

Huegel, F. T. *Bone of His Bone*. Grand Rapids, Mich.: Zondervan, 1980.

Jones, Russell Bradley. *Gold from Golgatha*. Chicago: Moody, 1945.

Kelly, Thomas. *A Testament of Devotion*. New York: Harper, 1941.

Kimmel, Tim. *Little House on the Freeway*. Portland, Oreg.: Multnomah, 1987. Quoted in *Focus on the Family Magazine*, February 1988, 3.

Laubach, Frank. *Letters of a Modern Mystic*. Old Tappan, N.J.: Felming H. Revell, n.d.

Law, William. *A Serious Call to a Devout and Holy Life*. Philadelphia: Westminster Press, 1948.

The Message of Keswick. New edition. London: Marshall, Morgan and Scott, 1957.

Miller, Calvin. *A Symphony in Sand*. Dallas. Word, 1990.

Murray, Andrew. *The Two Covenants*. Old Tappan, N.J.: Fleming H. Revell, 1974.

Nouwen, Henri J. M. *Making All Things New*. New York: Harper and Row, 1981.

Ortlund, Anne. *Building a Great Marriage*. Old Tappan, N.J.: Fleming H. Revell, 1985.

———. *Children Are Wet Cement*. Old Tappan, N.J.: Fleming H. Revell, 1981.

———. *Disciplines of the Beautiful Woman*. Waco, Tex.: Word, 1977.

———. *Disciplines of the Heart*. Waco, Tex.: Word, 1987.

———. *Disciplines of the Home*. Dallas: Word, 1990.

———. *Discipling One Another*. Waco, Tex.: Word, 1979. Originally published as *Love Me with Tough Love*.

———. *Fix Your Eyes on Jesus*. Dallas: Word, 1991.

———. *Joanna: A Story of Renewal*. Waco, Tex.: Word, 1982. Originally published as *The Acts of Joanna*.

———. *Up with Worship*. Glendale, Calif.: Regal, 1975.

Ortlund, Raymond, and Anne Ortlund. *Confident in Christ*. Portland, Oreg.: Multnomah, 1989.

————. *You Don't Have to Quit*. Nashville: Thomas Nelson, 1986. Originally published as *Staying Power*.

Women's Devotional Bible. Grand Rapids, Mich.: Zondervan, 1990.

Sanders, Oswald. *Christ Incomparable*. Fort Washington, Pa.: Christian Literature Crusade, 1952.

————. *Spiritual Maturity*. Chicago: Moody Press, 1962.

Smith, Hannah Whitall. *The Christian's Secret of a Happy Life*. 1870. Reprint. Westwood, N.J.: Barbour, 1985.

Sproul, R. C. *One Holy Passion*. Nashville: Thomas Nelson, 1987.

Spurgeon, Charles Haddon. *The Treasury of the New Testament*, vol. 3. Grand Rapids, Mich.: Zondervan, 1950.

Stewart, James. *A Man in Christ*. New York: Harper and Row, n.d.

Tozer, A. W. *Still Waters, Deep Waters*. Edited by Rowland Croucher. Sydney, Australia: Albatross, 1987.

————. "The Editorial Voice." *The Alliance Weekly*, 6 March 1963.

————. *The Pursuit of God*. Harrisburg, Pa.: Christian Publications, 1948.

Underhill, Evelyn, *Mount of Purification*. London: Longman, Green, 1960.

Wallis, Arthur. *In the Day of Thy Power*. Fort Washington, Pa.: Christian Literature Crusade, 1956.

Index of Subjects

276

Scripture Index